Every Bone Tells a Story

Hominin Discoveries, Deductions, and Debates

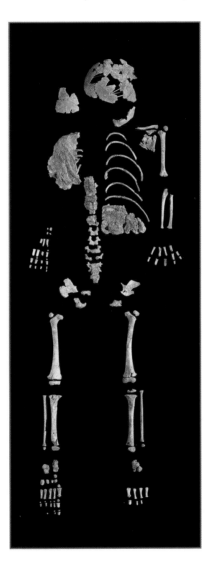

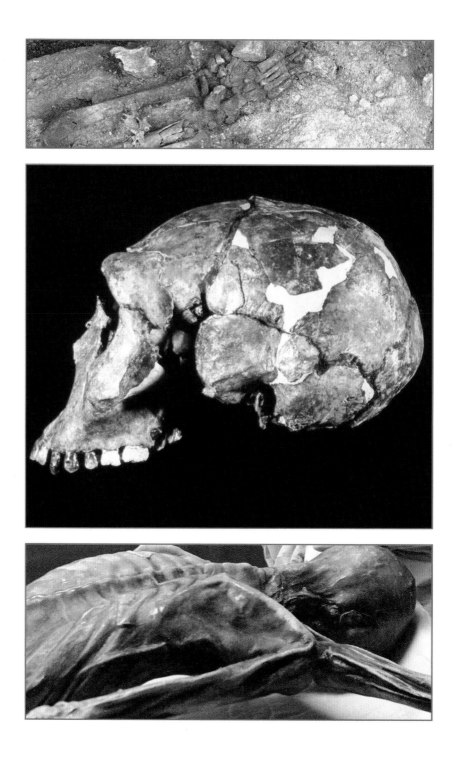

Every Bone Tells a Story

Hominin Discoveries, Deductions, and Debates

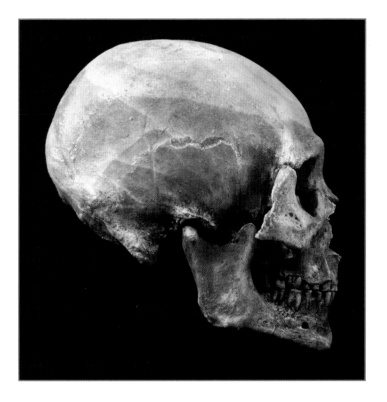

Jill Rubalcaba and Peter Robertshaw

i**≈**i Charlesbridge

To four very special hominins: Simon and Mia, Kelly and Daniel—P. R. and J. R.

Published by Charlesbridge
85 Main Street
Watertown, MA 02472
(617) 926-0329
www.charlesbridge.com

Library of Congress Cataloging-in-Publication Data
Rubalcaba, Jill.
    Every bone tells a story: Hominin discoveries, deductions, and debates / Jill Rubalcaba and Peter Robertshaw.
       p. cm.
    ISBN 978-1-58089-164-6 (reinforced for library use)
1. Fossil hominids—Juvenile literature. 2. Human remains (Archaeology)—Juvenile literature. 3. Prehistoric peoples—Juvenile literature. 4. Excavations (Archaeology)—Juvenile literature. 5. Archaeology—Case studies—Juvenile literature. 6. Archaeologists—Biography—Juvenile literature. 7. Archaeology—Philosophy—Juvenile literature. I. Robertshaw, Peter. II. Title.
GN282.5.R83 2010
930.1—dc22   2008026961

Printed in Singapore
(hc) 10 9 8 7 6 5 4 3 2 1

Display type and text type set in Poster Bodoni and Century Schooolbook
Printed and bound September 2009 by Imago in Singapore
Production supervision by Brian G. Walker
Designed by Susan Mallory Sherman

Table of Contents

Highlighted are the places in which each hominin was discovered:
Washington State (Kennewick Man), Portugal (Lapedo Child),
Italy (Iceman), and Kenya (Turkana Boy).

Introduction

Most people think the dead are silent, but to an archaeologist they're boisterous storytellers. Favorite tales come from remains thousands, even millions, of years old. Of course the dead don't leap out of their graves and give away their secrets. It takes scientists from every field imaginable to coax the details out of them. The stories are often garbled, and scientists don't always agree about what the dead are saying. And then sometimes another find comes along with a different version of the story that changes everything.

A hundred years ago archaeologists were adventurers with a splash of scientist in their blood. They were driven to find *things* from the past—grand things, like treasures and kings. In the last century archaeology has changed dramatically. Today's archaeologists are scientists first and foremost. They are driven to find out *about* things from the past—often ordinary things belonging to ordinary people.

These are the tales of four ordinary people—four hominins who lived long before recorded history. Although not long ago we would have called these four relatives of ours "hominids," researchers recently began calling humans and their ancestors by the more precise term "hominin." Join those researchers and archaeologists, along with scores of scientists in the discovery and recovery of these four hominins. Find out how scientists have expanded on what was learned in the field during the dig and what they've been able to deduce from each set of remains in the laboratory. Take a stand in the debates those deductions ignited. These three Ds in archaeology—discovery, deductions, and debates—help scientists develop a picture of how people lived in the past.

We begin where it began for all hominins—in Africa. To be a member of our primate family, Hominidae, you must walk on two legs, and 1.6 million years ago Turkana Boy did just that. But did he speak? Turkana Boy, the most complete *Homo erectus* skeleton found to date in fossil-rich East Africa, sparked the questions, When did language begin? And why did we start talking?

We know hominins got their start in Africa, but what was our ancestors' next move? How did they populate the world? The unusual anatomy of Portugal's Lapedo Child spiced up several hot archaeological debates. Who walked out of Africa, and what happened once they did? On what twig of the evolutionary "bush" does the Neandertal sit? As hominins evolved, were there crossovers between species that would explain Lapedo Child's mixed features? If Lapedo Child is part Neandertal, are you?

Populating the world was no easy task. There were those pesky oceans to cross to get to the Americas—or were there alternate routes? Kennewick Man, discovered in Washington State by students, instigated a battle that would make headlines for years. What did the modern humans who migrated to North America look like? How did they get here? Who can you claim as your ancestor, anyhow?

Tracing ancestry genetically began with Iceman. Due to a fortunate sequence of climatic events, Iceman came to scientists from a glacier in the Italian Alps with his soft tissue intact and his belongings preserved. Scientists worked to reconstruct an Alpine environment from 5,000 years ago and discovered a picture of modern humans on the move. DNA from Iceman's living European descendants inspired a new way of looking at how farmers and agriculture spread into Europe. In a "which came first, the chicken or the egg?" debate, scientists grappled over the question, Which came first to Europe—the farmer or farming practices?

The remains of four ordinary people engaged thousands of scientific minds to produce countless deductions, which have fueled endless fiery debates. Not so ordinary, after all.

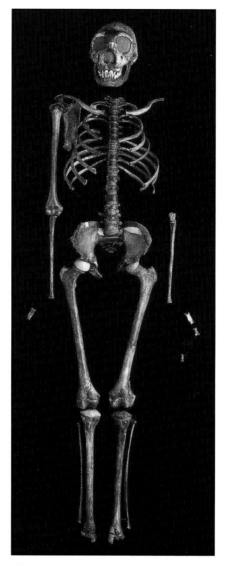

This reconstructed skeleton of Turkana Boy is the most complete example of a single *Homo erectus* individual yet discovered.

Turkana Boy
Discovery

1.6 million years ago . . .

The boy died facedown in a shallow lagoon. His body bobbed gently in the near motionless water close to the shore. Sand washed over him. Days turned into weeks; his flesh rotted. Months turned into years; his teeth fell out and collected in the cup of an animal's hoofprint. A hippo tromping through the shallows stepped on the boy's right leg bone, snapping it in two. Once flesh and muscle and ligament were gone, the bones separated. The lighter ones floated to shore. The lower jaw separated from the skull. The cranium rolled away, settling upside down in the muck. What was left of the boy disappeared under the silt.

Years turned into centuries, and centuries turned into millennia, while grain by grain, minerals in the sand replaced minerals in the bones, turning the bones into solid rock.

While the boy's fossilized bones remained buried, the world above changed. A drier climate transformed the landscape. The lush tropical vegetation the boy had known faded away. Where trees once wove canopies above thriving grasses, isolated weeds struggled to survive. What was once moist and green turned parched and brown. Any plant scrappy enough to grow had thorns, as if a prickly nature were necessary to survive. Unchecked rainwater cut gullies that sliced through ancient sediments, creating walls rippling with cream, red, and tangerine.

Wind and the rare downpour peeled off layers of sand and sediment, and the boy's 1.6-million-year-old fossilized bones began to surface. Just a foot below the parched ground, the boy's sand-filled cranium held precious drops of water and became a pot for a seed. A wait-a-bit thorn tree sprouted. For 20 years the thorny tree grew. The roots snaked through the plates in the brain case and shattered the cranium. Some of the bone fragments drifted free of the roots' clutches. One tiny piece of skull poked through the pebbles.

West Turkana, Kenya, August 1984 . . .

For two weeks fossil hunters known as the Hominid Gang had worked without a break. These six fossil hunters, who had been together long before the term "hominin" had come into fashion, were trained and led by a stocky Kenyan, Kamoya Kimeu. Together they walked the lunarlike landscape. They scrambled up slopes scattered with loose pebbles, snaked the ridge-tops, catching a breeze, then dipped back into the 135-degree heat of the airless gullies. Behind them they left almost no cairns, rock piles built to mark the location of a fossil find. They'd found no hominin fossils at all— no traces of humans or human ancestors anywhere. To them this was failure. They were tired. They were discouraged. It was time to move on.

During the worst of the midday heat, the Hominid Gang set up their next camp alongside a river of sand called the Nariokotome. The first thing they did was look for water. They had to dig deeper than the year before, but they found it. Then on the bank of the dry riverbed, in the spotty shade of the acacia trees, they pitched their canvas tents. Although they couldn't see Lake Turkana, three miles east of camp, they could make out the faint scent of the lake's rotting algae on the breeze, mixed with the closer, stronger smells of goat herds, burned grass, and sunbaked dirt.

In the intense midday heat, the bustling camp sounds—the clatter of pots and pans, the slosh of water for dishes and baths and laundry, the sound of shovels striking rock and sand—had quieted to soft restful murmurs, the even rhythms of snores, the gentle *flap, flap* of laundry drying in the breeze, and the *scratch, scratch, scratch* of pencil on paper as a few fossil hunters wrote letters home.

But Kimeu couldn't relax. Frustration prickled his normally even nature. After two weeks of staring at the ground hour after hour, day after day, they had found nothing hominin. Not even a tooth. Why hadn't they found even a sliver of hominin bone? Would their new location alongside the Nariokotome be any better? Leaving his fellow fossil hunters behind to rest, Kimeu decided to relieve his itchiness with a walk.

Heading south from camp, he shuffled down the pebbled bank of the Nariokotome, scanning the ground for fossils. He crossed the roadlike riverbed and scrambled up the other bank, following a well-worn goat path. The path wound near a small acacia tree and a large *Salvadora* tree. This wasn't a good place to find fossils. The ground had been trampled by camels and goats and the young boys who herded them. But Kimeu looked anyhow. He was 300 yards south of camp when he spotted it.

Almost anyone else would have walked right by without seeing it. But Kimeu was not almost anyone. He was a fossil hunter—the best there was. The small chunk of cranium, no bigger than a matchbook, looked just like the lava pebbles that surrounded it. Its surface was covered with pinhole pits, hairwidth scars, and sand-grain-sized bumps. But Kimeu knew—even before he picked it up—that this was hominin.

When he rubbed it between his thumb and forefinger, he felt the thick concave curve of bone that had once protected a brain. Not the small brain of an antelope or a gazelle or a pig—the big brain belonging to a hominin. From his many years of field experience, he knew that this curve belonged to the skull of *Homo erectus,* the hominin that lived before modern humans. Turkana Boy had surfaced.

Back at camp Kimeu and the fossil hunters removed the battery from the Land Rover and hooked it up to the radio telephone. The signal was so weak that Kimeu had to yell into the receiver. The operator connected him to anthropologist Richard Leakey, who was working at the museum in Nairobi, cleaning fossils. They had found something, Kimeu hollered into the radio telephone. They had finally found something. Perhaps Leakey would like to come see?

"Keep them safe for me, and we'll see you tomorrow," Leakey replied.

❖ ❖ ❖

Richard Leakey's friend and colleague, anthropologist Alan Walker, happened to be in Nairobi working with Leakey when Kimeu called. Walker, curious to see Kimeu's find, packed up the fossils he'd been studying and joined Leakey. They loaded Leakey's single-engine Cessna with supplies and topped off the wing tanks with fuel. Once airborne, Leakey banked the Cessna north toward Lake Turkana, Kamoya Kimeu, the Hominid Gang, and that tiny scrap of Turkana Boy's cranium.

Two hours into the flight, they reached the southern tip of Lake Turkana. The lake shimmered below them. Wind skim-

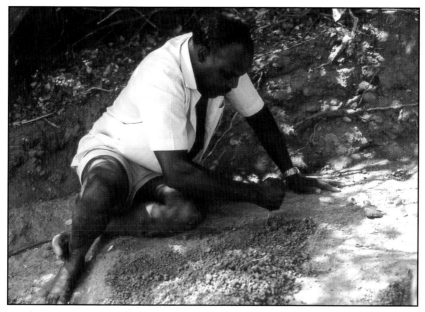

Kamoya Kimeu, head of the Hominid Gang, breaks hard-packed topsoil with a pick. This arduous task must be performed cautiously to prevent damaging the delicate fossils located beneath the surface.

ming the lake shifted the floating algae, turning the water from blue gray to jade green and back again. The brilliant jade looked all the more vibrant alongside the dull mud banks. From the air the banks looked like thick brown paint that children had run their fingers through—those finger tracks were crocodile slides.

The Hominid Gang had cleared an airstrip—a very *short* airstrip. Leakey liked them as short as possible to keep out unwanted guests. Approaching the strip, Leakey slowed the plane to just a few miles above stall speed. The slower he came in, the quicker he could come to a stop. At 1,500 feet the stall warning bleated. Leakey lifted the nose, stalling just as the tires hit the ground with a thud. The Cessna bounced, once, twice, and then settled into a shudder as the plane rumbled against the hard brake.

When Leakey threw open the cockpit window, the men were torched by hot desert air perfumed with goat dung. "OK, Walker. Let's see what they got for us this time."

❖ ❖ ❖

In *The Wisdom of Bones,* Alan Walker wrote, "Our hearts sank when we saw the small fossil, a rectangular piece about one inch by two inches, and the wretched little slope on the opposite side of the river." Richard Leakey wrote in his field diary that night, "Seldom have I seen anything less hopeful." But in the world of paleoanthropology, even the bleakest lead is followed. So after dinner, in a mess tent lit by lantern light, Leakey and Walker planned the excavation.

In the morning the Hominid Gang cleared the area of debris. The fossil hunters picked up leaves, twigs, pebbles, and rocks. Once the slope was clear, the gang broke up the hard-packed top layer of dirt with Olduvai picks. These tools, made from two-inch nails sticking out of carved wooden handles, fit neatly into the palms of the excavators' hands. With a steady *thwack, thwack, thwack,* the Hominid Gang broke up the crusted surface. The locals Leakey had hired to help with the excavation swept the loosened sediment, called backdirt, into metal bowls. Schoolboys, working to earn extra money, dumped the backdirt into wheelbarrows and wheeled it to the sieves.

The sieves are two-by-three-foot wooden frames with two layers of mesh attached to the bottom. The coarser layer is like chicken wire, metal with quarter-inch holes. The finer layer is similar to mosquito netting. Workers sift the sediment with a back-and-forth motion. When all the dirt has been reduced to dust and fallen away, what's left bounces on top of the mesh. The sievers examine each piece carefully, looking for bones or teeth. Sieving is hot, dusty, tedious, exhausting work.

Neither Walker nor Leakey believed anything would come of the small scrap of skull. Whether or not Kimeu believed there was more to be found, he didn't say. He kept at the grueling work of breaking up the soil, carting it to the sievers, sifting and sorting—and finding nothing. Walker and Leakey began looking for excuses to escape. Even the prospect of checking out stromatolites, a kind of fossilized algae on the shore of Lake Turkana, was more appealing to them than the dust storm at the site, so off they went. Kimeu and the rest of the Hominid Gang continued to work.

The dust-covered workers paused now and again to laugh at the Turkana children, who were playing not far from the site in a *Salvadora* tree. Hidden inside the tree's tent of leaves, the children squealed and giggled. When the children plucked the *Salvadora*'s sweet-sour berries to munch on, the leaves quivered. The tree looked comical to the workers, as if it were shaking with its own belly laughs.

Kimeu's amused smile at the playful children broadened into a wide grin when he looked down and noticed in the soft dirt at his feet, among the surface stones, a piece of skull . . . and then another . . . and another.

When Leakey and Walker returned to camp late that afternoon, the fossil hunters came running. "We've found more bone! Lots of skull!" The anthropologists jumped out of the Land Rover and ran, in Leakey's words, "to where Kamoya was sitting, his treasure arrayed before him, like jewels plucked from the earth."

Suddenly that miserable scrap of skull didn't seem so

hopeless. Within the week the crew recovered many skull and facial bones. It was time to call their sponsor, the National Geographic Society. National Geographic sent photographer David Brill to the excavation. Walker wrote in *The Wisdom of the Bones* that when Brill arrived he began taking photographs "like a demented grasshopper, all elbows and long legs, contorting this way and that to get the best photographic angle."

Leaving Brill to photograph what they had excavated so far, Leakey climbed into his Cessna to fetch his wife, Meave Leakey, and their daughters, Louise and Samira. While Leakey was gone, Walker continued the sieving. The dust choked the workers and coated their bodies. Walker decided that sieving under the camp shower would be more efficient and less annoying.

The hired schoolboys trundled the backdirt over to the camp "shower," which was nothing more than a canvas bag with a showerhead attached, hanging from a tree. The water dissolved the dirt, carrying it through the mesh in the sieves, leaving the larger bits and pieces behind. Once the fossils had been rinsed of the clingy black lava dust, their natural reddish brown color appeared—a burnished mahogany.

It wasn't long before Leakey's Cessna touched down again. Leakey's daughters jumped out. Louise, who was 12 years old, planned to learn to drive the Land Rover. Samira, who was two years younger, had agreed to come along and help as long as Dad promised to splash her with water whenever she got too hot.

Meave Leakey headed right for the table where Walker had laid out the dozen or so scraps of skull. The two of them set to gluing the pieces together. Putting a skull back together is a lot like working on a three-dimensional puzzle. Walker and Meave Leakey each had loved puzzles when they

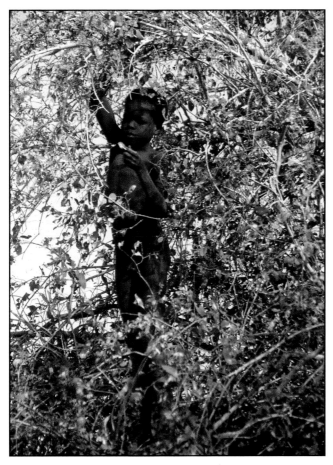

A Turkana child eats fruit while balanced in the branches of the *Salvadora* (toothbrush tree) that hangs over the excavation.

were children, but found them much too easy. To make the puzzles more challenging, they both had flipped the pieces upside down and put the puzzles together without any help from a picture. This unusual method for piecing puzzles turned out to be terrific training for reconstructing a cranium—piecing shattered bone together by shape. Now, sitting in the shade, the two turned scraps of skull this way and that until a fit became clear.

That night at dinner Walker told Brill that skulls speak to those who listen. He claimed that after a lifetime of searching for them, piecing them together, and marveling over them, one begins to hear what they are saying. The Hominid Gang joked that the bones speak in Kikichwa—the language of the skulls.

Brill turned to Kimeu and asked if he could hear the skulls speak. Was that why Kimeu found more hominin bones than anyone else? Did the bones whisper to him, "Come here . . . look here?" Kimeu said that the skulls did speak to him, and then he stopped for a moment to think. "But you can't understand them!"

On the banks of the Nariokotome, the bones spoke to them all. The excitement in camp generated a current that could have powered a city. Then suddenly the bones were silent. The discoveries stopped. The workers started at dawn, dug and sieved relentlessly for three hours, but found nothing more than a yellow scorpion.

Richard Leakey circled a wait-a-bit thorn tree, careful not to snag his clothing and get caught in the trap that gives the tree its name. "Walker, if there's nothing more after this, we'll call it quits," he said. He looked thoughtfully at the thorny tree and then tossed a green cushion onto the ground next to it. He sat on the cushion, leaning back a bit, looking as if he were sitting in a washbasin. He traded an Olduvai pick for a four-inch paintbrush and worked carefully around the roots of the tree.

Cramped from sitting with no back support, Richard Leakey stood, took off his shirt and hung it on a branch, traded in the paintbrush for a dental pick, and then went back to

Kamoya Kimeu and Alan Walker search for bone fragments near the dried up riverbed of Nariokotome.

work, lying on his stomach with his face just inches from the tree roots.

Nearby, Walker said to no one in particular, "Listen for the ping; when you hit bone, it sounds different."

The workers sang an English song taught in the Turkana schools. The children in the *Salvadora* tree on the opposite riverbank leaned this way and that to make the tree sway to the beat of the chorus, singing back, "I want, I want . . . to be, to be. . . ."

The sandstone quickly dulled the workers' Olduvai picks. But no one complained. Sharpening the points gave the diggers' knees a break.

"I want, I—"

From his prone position, Richard Leakey shouted for the

Richard Leakey gets comfortable during the dig. Excavating in the African heat can be exhausting. Workers often take breaks and will seek shade to rest during the hottest part of the day.

others to come quickly. The singing stopped. He'd found a jaw stuck in the roots—an upper jaw with two gleaming teeth. The tree roots had not only broken the cranium apart, they had also snaked their way around and through Turkana Boy's face, breaking it apart, too. Now it would be up to Meave Leakey and Walker to put it back together again.

Meave Leakey and Walker leaned over the new fragments, which were laid out on the worktable. They noticed that the teeth were the first two molars. There were no sockets for wisdom teeth. Did this jaw belong to an adolescent?

Samira and Louise had been hanging on the backs of the chairs, watching their mother and Walker. They all looked over to the excavation site a few feet away, where Richard Leakey was still working, and decided to have a bit of fun. They'd carry a message to their father the African way. They wrote a note: "The gluing team got smart and counted teeth. It's a sub-adult!"

Samira trotted over to her dad with the note stuck into a cleft stick.

❖ ❖ ❖

It wasn't long into the digging season when they all realized this "sub-adult" was something extraordinary. Until Turkana Boy, only bits and pieces of *Homo erectus* had been discovered. Almost everything that Walker and Richard Leakey uncovered was a first. "This is the first clavicle of *Homo erectus* known to science," Walker would say, turning the find over with wonder. "This is the first lumbar vertebra of a *Homo erectus* known to science."

Every hour they uncovered fossils that ordinarily would have made an entire digging season a smashing success. It became so routine that Brill stopped taking pictures. Walker scolded him, "The first thoracic vertebra of *Homo erectus* you've seen, anyone's seen, and only the second pelvis ever seen—*and you're not taking pictures!*"

They were so close to a complete skeleton that they decided to enlarge the excavation in hopes of finding all of Turkana Boy. The Hominid Gang wouldn't let Richard Leakey and Walker pickax the soil above the fossil layer. It may seem as though it takes nothing more than brute strength to break up that top layer, but with precious "firsts" just below the surface, it's critical to have a skilled touch—and Walker and Richard Leakey weren't good enough at it. After the top layers, or overburden, had been precisely removed, more bones appeared—ribs, a lower leg bone, the sacrum.

By now another Leakey had joined the excavation—

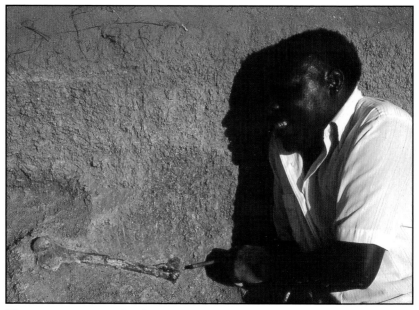

Kimeu examines a leg bone (femur) embedded in the packed dirt. It will be his job to help remove the bone without damaging it.

Richard's mother, Mary. She sat in the shade, scolding her son for the sloppiness of the hole compared to her meticulous digs at Olduvai Gorge—the archaeologist mother's equivalent of "your room is a mess." Despite his mother's teasing, he knew she shared his excitement. Fossil hunters and archaeologists are no different when it comes to the thrill of the find.

Meave Leakey and Walker continued to piece bones together—no longer merely a chunk of cranium and a tooth, but almost an entire skeleton. And the Leakey girls continued to hang on the backs of their chairs, sharing the shade.

Walker said to Samira, "Give me your finger." When she held out her finger, he stuck it into a thimblelike hollow on Turkana Boy's left temple. "Do you know what that is?"

Samira shook her head.

He told her that it was "the region of the brain that controls the muscles you use in speaking."

Samira snatched her hand away and giggled. She and Louise ran to tell their dad. Their mother and Walker smiled when they heard the girls say, "The boy could talk!"

❖ ❖ ❖

Meave Leakey and Walker looked at one another. They had no idea what Turkana Boy would have said 1.6 million years ago, but they knew that for years to come, he'd be saying quite a lot.

Deductions
Turkana Boy

By September 1988 the digging was done. The light bones of Turkana Boy's hands and feet were most likely dispersed far and wide. To search for them the team would have to level the entire hillside. There simply wasn't enough money for that extensive an excavation, particularly with the very real possibility that they would come up empty-handed.

Alan Walker and Richard Leakey moved Turkana Boy to a museum lab in Nairobi, where team members cleaned his remains using dental picks and air scribes under the magnification of binocular microscopes. The team numbered and cataloged the hundreds of bone fragments. Walker measured and wrote up descriptions of each piece.

As much as Richard Leakey wanted to be involved in this phase of Turkana Boy's journey—where questions were finally answered—his beloved Africa needed him more. Poachers were slaughtering elephants by the thousands. Even the most complete *Homo erectus* ever found couldn't keep Richard Leakey in the lab. He went to work as director of the Wildlife Service in Kenya. He fired corrupt rangers, then hired and trained 4,500 new ones. He raised money. He lobbied for new laws. Turkana Boy had waited 1.6 million years. The elephants of Africa couldn't wait another moment.

But Walker wouldn't face Turkana Boy's questions alone. He put together a team of young scientists. He wanted young minds that weren't attached to old theories or stuck in traditional thinking. These bright young men and women brought new approaches and fresh ideas to the questions Turkana Boy raised. One of the first questions they tackled was . . .

How old was Turkana Boy?

On television the medical examiner always announces the victim's age with great precision. So how old would a medical examiner say Turkana Boy was when he died? The answer isn't as clear-cut as you might imagine. His age depends on what Turkana Boy was most like—a human, an ape, or a monkey. Humans, apes, and monkeys all grow in the same way, but they grow at different rates. They reach the same milestones at different ages.

Teeth are great markers for the different stages of development. We all have that same first-grade picture—the one with the gap-toothed grin, where those two front teeth have fallen out. Scientists mark the end of infancy with the eruption of the first set of permanent molars. The second set of permanent molars (the 12-year molars) mark the beginning of adolescence. When the wisdom teeth break the gum, it's the beginning of adulthood. Walker knew that Turkana Boy had his first two sets of molars but no sockets for wisdom teeth. Now he had to match Turkana Boy's growth to the appropriate model.

Monkeys have the fastest growth rates. They reach each milestone at very young ages; much too young for Turkana Boy. So the scientists set aside that model. That left human and ape models. After comparing teeth growth rates in human and ape models (see chart on page 22), the scientists found that Turkana Boy didn't match either model, but he fell somewhere in between.

GROWTH MARKER	HUMANS	CHIMPS (APE MODEL CHOSEN)
End of Infancy	6 years	3 years 4 months
Beginning of Adolescence	12 years	6 years 6 months
Beginning of Adulthood	18 years	11 years 5 months

Walker and his team examined the tops of the molars. Did the molars show any wear? If so, how much? No wear would mean the molar had not yet broken through the gum. Slight wear would mean it had been exposed for a short time. The amount of wear on Turkana Boy's molars told the scientists that he was a young adolescent.

Just like on television, real-life forensic scientists measure bones to make deductions about the victim. Walker and his team turned to Turkana Boy's bones for more information. The ends of the bones in your arms and legs continue to grow longer as you grow taller. While you're growing, the ends are cartilage—they don't turn into bone until you're about 16 or 17. When the cartilage turns to bone, the bones stop getting longer, and the ends show a closure called epiphyseal fusion.

Walker looked at the ends of Turkana Boy's bones to see where the cartilage had started to turn to bone and where it had not. None of Turkana Boy's arm and leg bones had completed the fusion process, but the elbow end of his arm bone had begun to fuse. In a human the fusion would begin around 11 years old. So according to a human model, Turkana Boy must have been at least 11 (because the fusion had started), but not yet 16 (because Turkana Boy's end bones were still cartilage).

Trying to narrow that age range even further, Walker examined Turkana Boy's hipbone. He found no fusion at all. If Turkana Boy was human and 13 years old, Walker would have seen the beginnings of epiphyseal fusion in the hipbone. So Walker knew that Turkana Boy was younger than 13 (and older than 11).

Walker hoped Turkana Boy's skull would have more answers. Like teeth, brain size is a marker for age. Turkana Boy's skull protected an 880-cubic-centimeter brain. By adding this fact to the rest of the data—the teeth, the epiphyseal fusion—Walker and his team estimated that Turkana Boy was a young adolescent who died when he was between 65 to 75 percent of his way to adulthood. If he was human that would make him 12 or 13. If he was a chimp, he'd be around 7. But Turkana Boy was neither human nor chimp; he was from an extinct species, a human ancestor called *Homo erectus*. The team decided that the evidence present in Turkana Boy's bones indicated that he had died when he was between 9 and 10 years old.

So why did Turkana Boy die so young? Nine-year-olds don't keel over in the water and drop dead. The scientists didn't believe he was attacked by a predator. There were no teeth marks on his skeleton to indicate a violent death. Walker x-rayed Turkana Boy's jaw and found evidence of an infection. Walker suspected that, a few weeks before Turkana Boy died, he yanked out a baby tooth that wasn't ready to drop out. The tooth's roots left two tiny tunnels into his gum—an open pathway for bacteria. The bacteria caused an infection. The infection led to an abscess.

Today all we would have to do is take some penicillin and within 24 hours the infection would be on the mend, but for Turkana Boy there was no magic pill. Abscessed teeth were deadly. In fact, until a few hundred years ago, tooth abscesses were second only to the plague as the leading cause of death. It's possible that, with his jaw aching horribly, a feverish

Turkana Boy stumbled to the water's edge, fell facedown in the water, and died.

What did Turkana Boy look like?

He was tall. Walker had known this when he first saw Turkana Boy's leg bone back at the excavation—it was long. For a rough estimate, he had held it up to the schoolboys who were working the site. Some of the older boys weren't as tall as Turkana Boy had been.

In the lab Walker compared the length of the upper leg bone to the length of the lower leg bone to calculate an accurate height. Turkana Boy was five feet three inches tall. Or perhaps an inch or two shorter, since humans have a domed skull and *Homo erectus* did not. Still, at 9 years old, that's quite tall. If Turkana Boy had lived to become a full-grown man he would have been at least six feet one inch tall.

Walker calculated that Turkana Boy had weighed about 106 pounds when he died and would have weighed 150 pounds when fully grown. This was not the body image scientists had in mind when they first pictured *Homo erectus*. Where was the short, stocky, muscle-bound ancestor that scientists had come to expect of early hominins? Hominins got taller and taller and taller through their evolutionary history, didn't they?

Turkana Boy's height may have been due to what *Homo erectus* ate. *Homo erectus* didn't farm. He roamed the landscape, eating whatever was available. That doesn't sound very healthy to us, but depending on farming for your diet isn't good for your health. It limits the variety of foods you eat, and a limited diet stunts your growth. Farming is necessary to support large numbers of people, but it doesn't support them as well as a hunter-gatherer's diet can. When humans began farming, average heights dropped.

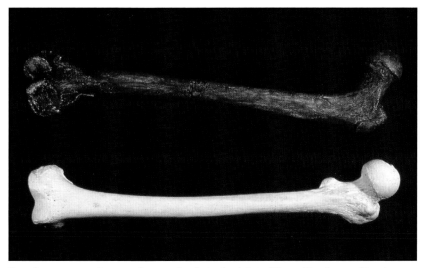

Leg bones can be used to calculate height. Here Turkana Boy's upper leg bone, or femur (top), is being compared to that of a modern human (bottom) in order to show the long neck on the *Homo erectus* bone (the area between the head, or ball, at the right end and the knobs at the bottom of the shaft). The long neck is associated with muscle/bone relationships that are slightly different from the modern human pattern.

Even though Turkana Boy's beanpole build was a surprise, it made sense. Height and body shape adapt to the environment, especially to temperature. Think of how you lie in your bed on a cold night. You curl up in a fetal position to keep warm. But on a hot night, you stretch out as long as possible on your bed. That exposes the largest area of skin to the air in order to cool you. Tall, slender bodies get along better in hot dry climates than short, stocky builds. In cold climates a short, stocky build has the advantage. It holds on to heat.

Turkana Boy had lived in a hot climate, and it looked as though he may have sweated. His ancestors, the hominins that came before him, had had fur. They would have needed to pant like furry animals do. Instead, Turkana Boy could have kept cool by sweating, just like humans do.

The nasal opening in Turkana Boy's skull indicated that, like humans, he had a nose—a real nose. Hominins before *Homo erectus* had flat noses like apes. Their nostrils sank into their faces. *Homo erectus's* nose stuck out. This new and improved design saved moisture—another advantage in a hot climate. When Turkana Boy breathed in, his nostrils moisturized the air as it traveled to his lungs. When Turkana Boy breathed out, his nostrils saved some of that moisture before it was lost to the hot dry air. By conserving moisture Turkana Boy could run, climb, dig, and scavenge—even during the hottest part of the day when all the other animals were napping in the shade.

Walker noticed that the part of Turkana Boy's leg bone where muscle attaches was much thicker than in a strong human. We know that bones change according to the amount of stress put on them. Sit around all day, and your bones get thin. Run and jump and lift weights, and your bones build up to support those extra-strong muscles. Turkana Boy's muscles must have worked hard to make such thick bones.

Recently a scientist demonstrated how activity can thicken bones. For his test subjects he chose armadillos because they have litters of four genetically identical young. The scientist let two of the armadillos do the armadillo thing—digging and napping. He took the other two to the gym. Those two ran on treadmills. The gym armadillos' bones grew thicker. Judging by the thickness of Turkana Boy's bones, he had superhuman strength.

Walker wanted to look into Turkana Boy's face. Normally scientists make a cast of the skull and then press clay onto the cast, sculpting a face. But Walker wasn't satisfied with a

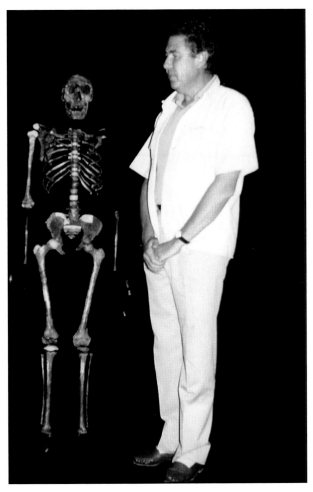

Alan Walker stands next to the skeleton of
Turkana Boy. For a 9-year-old, Turkana Boy was
quite tall.

mere glimpse of Turkana Boy on the last day of his life. He
wanted to see what *Homo erectus* looked like at 9 years old
and as he got older.

Walker expanded his team to include an expert on how
skulls change as a person ages. The expert planned to take

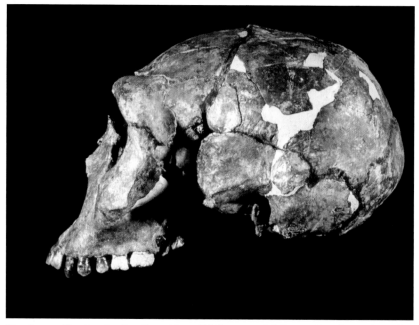

Turkana Boy's skull after Alan Walker and Maeve Leakey pieced the bone fragments together and glued them in place.

measurements of Turkana Boy's skull and then connect those points to an adult *Homo erectus* face. The only problem was that no one had ever found an adult male's face. There was, however, one adult female face. Taking into account the differences between how males and females mature, the expert worked on a mug shot of Turkana Boy—one that aged.

In the meantime Walker made a cast of the *inside* of Turkana Boy's skull. Turkana Boy's brain was less than three-quarters the size of a human boy's, but it was bigger than the hominins that came before him. *Homo erectus* was smart enough to make tools, but not smart enough to make improvements on the tools. Tools stayed the same for hundreds of thousands of years.

The right side of Turkana Boy's brain was slightly wider and stuck out a bit more in the front. That detail, along with a longer right arm bone, told Walker that Turkana Boy was right-handed. But the thing that caused loud and long debates among anthropologists was evidence of one small bump on the left side of his brain. The bump is called Broca's area. It's named after Paul Broca, the doctor who put two and two together when he autopsied a man who had lost his ability to speak. Broca found tissue damage in the left front of the man's brain and determined that the bump had something to do with speech. It was clear that Turkana Boy's brain had Broca's area. Who would have thought a little bump could cause such a fuss? But when scholars started asking if Turkana Boy could talk, that little bump detonated explosive debates about the origins of language.

Debates
Turkana Boy

Did language begin long ago and develop slowly? Or did it begin recently and develop rapidly? If Turkana Boy proved that *Homo erectus* talked, then he would support the long-ago-and-slowly side of the debate.

Tracing the evolution of language turns out to be trickier than tracing the evolution of our species. Language doesn't fossilize. When *did* language begin? And what kicked it off?

Vocalizations: the animal connection

Looking for answers as to when language began, field biologists are listening to our ancestral sounds—wild-animal vocalizations.

Vervets, cat-sized monkeys, travel in groups throughout the forests of eastern Africa. They have a sophisticated communication system—their survival depends on it. A research team recorded vervet alarm calls. When they played back the vervet scream for "snake," the monkeys stood on hind legs, stretched their necks, and frantically scanned the ground. When the team played the call for "leopard," the vervets scampered up the nearest tree and clung onto branches too skimpy to support a big cat. And when the team played the "eagle" warning, the vervets dove for cover. These playback experiments clearly illustrated that vervets can communicate.

Further studies revealed that vervet calls don't bubble up

out of some primal instinct. They are learned communications. Baby vervets use the calls with little discrimination. They'll shout "eagle" when anything floats overhead—including leaves. But the youngsters quickly refine their calls. Soon they only yell "eagle" when there is a predatory bird soaring above them.

Linguists point out that although there are benefits to being able to identify where your attacker is coming from, single-word warnings do not qualify as "language." Language is the ability to string words together in complex sentences. Kanzi, a bonobo chimpanzee, is doing just that.

Psychologist Sue Savage-Rumbaugh spent years at the Language Research Center at Georgia State University trying to teach Matata, an adult female bonobo, words and symbols—unsuccessfully. During this time Matata had a baby named Kanzi. Savage-Rumbaugh said, "Kanzi would just be around. He would often be on my head, or jumping down from the top of the keyboard into my lap. If we asked Matata to sort objects, Kanzi would jump in the middle of them and mess them all up. So he was just a normal kid."

When Kanzi was two and a half, it was time for Matata to have another baby. The researchers took Matata away for breeding. Kanzi was devastated. He picked up Matata's keyboard (which she had never been good at using) and began selecting symbols. He wanted food. He wanted attention. Most of all Kanzi wanted his mother. Kanzi was communicating using the keyboard. He was stringing words together in complex sentences.

While taking long walks through the woods that surrounded the Language Research Center, Savage-Rumbaugh taught Kanzi hundreds of symbols. Kanzi learned to understand thousands of words. (Kanzi told Savage-Rumbaugh his favorite movie was *Iceman*.) Yet despite Kanzi's abilities, linguists refuse to say he uses "language."

Noam Chomsky, a linguist at Massachusetts Institute of Technology, compared trying to teach chimpanzees to speak to trying to teach people to fly. He said, "Humans can fly about 30 feet—that's what they do in the Olympics. Is that flying?"

Psychologist Steven Pinker agreed. He said, "No chimpanzee has learned sign language. They've certainly learned some gestures, but sign language is not just a system of gestures. It's a full grammatical language. . . ."

Compared to human communication, animal communication is simple and primitive. Linguists argue that grammar is the dividing line. Chimpanzees may be adept at communicating—for instance, communicating the desire for something to eat—but their word choices may flow something like: "Me banana want, you banana. Eat banana me."

Humans, on the other hand, are capable of rearranging a set of words to produce totally different meanings. For example, to us, "you took a bite out of my banana" is quite different from "my banana took a bite out of you."

It's our grammatical rules that allow us to decode the differences. Without grammar, linguists argue, there is no language. So, if animals don't have language, what stopped our ancestors from relying on animal sounds—barks, growls, hoots, and howls—and started them talking? And when?

Body parts: the anatomical connection

Soft tissues such as the vocal tract don't fossilize, but there are parts of the skeleton related to speech that do. The inner surface of the skull is covered with dents and ridges, lines and squiggles—impressions of the brain it once housed. By examining the skull's map left behind by the brain, scientists can determine if Turkana Boy had the brain parts necessary for speech.

The two sides of the brain work together to control different complicated tasks. One of those tasks is language. Broca's area, the area associated with the *production* of sound, is on the left side of the brain, toward the front, at about temple height. Without Broca's area you'd be able to understand what was being said to you, but you wouldn't be able to answer.

Above and behind the ear is another language-related section called Wernicke's area. Here speech is decoded and encoded. This area is associated with the *perception* of sound. Without Wernicke's area you wouldn't understand what was being said or be able to form a coherent answer. A nerve bundle, or neural pathway, connects Broca's area to Wernicke's area and controls the muscles that move your lips, tongue, jaw, and vocal cords.

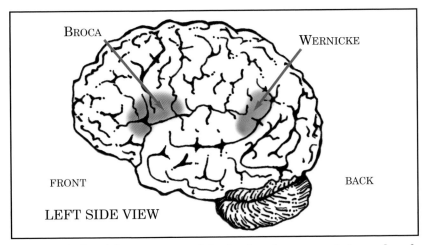

Broca and Wernicke are areas of the brain where speech is produced, processed, and comprehended. The two areas are connected by a bundle of nerves that control the mechanics of speech, including lip movement, tongue movement, and vocal cord vibration.

Another skeletal clue for speech lies in the neck. The voice box, or larynx, bulges out in the front of your neck in a bump some people call the Adam's apple. Cords inside the larynx control the pitch and volume of your voice.

The larynx has two possible positions in mammals. One position allows for full use of speech; the other for limited use. The latter position is high in the throat, allowing mammals to breathe and swallow at the same time. Not having to worry about choking is an advantage for survival, but this high position is a tight fit for the larynx. It restricts the vocal chords and limits sound production.

For full tonal range the larynx must sit low in the throat, where it can expand. Human voice boxes sit high for the first two years, which allows an infant to suckle efficiently. Then the larynx descends, reaching the adult position at about 14 years. (This is why boys' voices change about this time. The male throat is larger, which allows the male's larynx to expand more than the female's larynx and gives the male a deeper voice.) Mammal infant skulls (including human ones) are flat in the rear at the base, while adult human skulls flare to accommodate the lowering larynx.

Judging from other *Homo erectus* skulls, the position of the larynx in Turkana Boy's species was close to the position in modern humans. While scientists are certain that *Homo erectus* had Broca's area, measurements for Wernicke's area are inconclusive. But even if Turkana Boy had all the right equipment to speak, it doesn't mean that he did. Archaeologists continue to search sites where *Homo erectus* lived, looking for evidence of their possible use of language.

Tool talk

Some anthropologists argue that the manufacturing of tools is evidence of language. Their argument is that making tools to a preconceived shape rather than simply bashing a couple of rocks together to get a cutting edge requires some discussion about how to make the tools. Others argue that tool shapes are only similar because of the raw materials used. Different stones fracture differently—so the stone determined the tool. If you whack the edge of a particular piece of stone, then it's going to flake a particular way. There was no need to talk about it.

There are other anthropologists who link language and toolmaking, but they believe that hominins only needed to start talking when tools started to show variety. The debate is over how much variety requires speech. From 2.5 million years ago until about 250,000 years ago, tool design was pretty boring—the same old thing over and over again, with a change every million years or so. Around 250,000 years ago tool technology got innovative. Did language originate when changes in tool technology first appeared and spread? Or did it begin between 100,000 and 45,000 years ago, when tools became more complicated and specialized?

Art discussion

And then there are the scientists who say, "Forget the tools; look at the art." Language is essentially thinking in symbols. Art is symbolic expression. If language and art go hand in hand, then humans weren't carrying on conversations until about 35,000 years ago, when artistic expression blossomed.

Cave art has some of the most mysterious examples of symbolic art. There are rows of dots, zigzags, V shapes, and grids. What do they mean? Scholars have suggested everything from hunting directions to fertility rituals to the artist's signature. Regardless of what these geometric images mean, they are concrete evidence that humans were thinking symbolically.

First words

Stymied by the lack of definitive proof in bones and stones, scientists decided that if they could figure out *what* triggered the start of language, then they might have a better idea of *when* it began. What was it that started humans talking?

You would think that today's linguists, with their full capacity for language, would have come up with more scientific names for their theories, but clearly that's not the case. Here are a few of their theories about what started us jabbering:

The ouch theory

Language began when our ancestors cried out in pain ("ouch") and joy ("yippee") and surprise ("wow"). Our emotions led to sounds that led to language.

The bow-wow theory

Our ancestors were natural mimics. They copied the sounds around them—*bang, boom, bow-wow.* Over time the sounds became words and took on a broader meaning.

The yo-heave-ho theory

When a job requiring physical effort needed to get done, our ancestors chanted rhythmically to coordinate the effort. Think of a crew coxswain shouting, "Stroke, stroke, stroke" or sailors pulling on a line, yelling, "Heave-ho." The grunts from heavy work were the beginnings of communication.

The ta-ta theory

Before there were words, people communicated with gestures,

such as waving good-bye. Even today if you are trying to communicate with someone who doesn't speak English, you might resort to pantomime. Eventually vocal accompaniment of the movements evolved into language.

The ding-dong theory

Do the objects themselves suggest the sounds? Linguists have observed that in all languages there is a mysterious connection between certain sounds and their meanings. Small, fast, and sharp things have different sounds than big, slow, and round things. Compare the sounds of *tiny* to *enormous, razor* to *smooth, pinnacle* to *moon.* Big, slow, or round things tend to have rounded vowel sounds. And the opposite also tends to be true.

The la-la theory

Did we sing first? Chimps work themselves into a dither drumming, stomping, and waving branches to accompany their chorus. Were our first words lyrical rather than brutish grunts?

The goo-goo theory

This theory suggests that just as infants repeat the sounds they hear, when our ancestors began to talk, they repeated sounds on purpose until the other person understood.

The Mama-Dada theory (a refinement of the goo-goo theory)

Scholars who subscribe to this theory believe that language began much as it does for infants today—by assigning names to the people who are most important in their social group, such as their parents.

The ah-ha theory (also known as the eureka theory)

Perhaps language was invented. Some clever early humans

got it into their heads that if they assigned sounds to mean certain things, then they could communicate.

The hey you theory
Language arose out of the human need for identity and social contact. ("Hey you, it's me.")

The Pinocchio's nose theory
We can point and gesture, hoot and holler, to get our point across, but in order to lie, we need language. Was it our need to deceive that drove us to invent language?

The genetics of speech
These theories spawned some interesting debates, but they didn't pinpoint the *when,* as scientists had hoped. With DNA fast becoming the place to look for answers, scientists turned to genetics in hopes of getting a date.

All living things carry DNA. DNA is an organism's master plan—building instructions that have been passed down from generation to generation. All this necessary information for growth and function comes packed in every cell's nucleus. DNA is arranged in a formation that looks like a twisted ladder.

You would think that for performing such a complicated task as building a living thing and making it function, DNA would look like an undecipherable mathematical equation. It actually is quite simple. A DNA sequence is made up of only four different building blocks: C, G, A, and T. They work like an anagram. For example, even though "schoolmaster" and "the classroom" are composed of the same set of letters, they are two very different things. DNA codes work the same way.

Each sequence of letters is a set of instructions called a gene. A single strand of DNA contains many genes. If you were to pull a strand of DNA out of one of your cells, it would be as tall as you are. Fitting long strands inside the cell's nucleus requires efficient packing, and so the strands are compressed into units called chromosomes. A mosquito has 6 chromosomes, wheat has 14, a sunflower 34, a cat 38, a human 46, an elephant 56, and a dog 78.

The entire package—the information provided by all of the DNA in all of the gene sequences tied together in all of the chromosomes of any individual—is called a genome. Simply put, the genome is divided into chromosomes, chromosomes contain genes, and genes are made of DNA.

The human genome is made up of 3 billion of those genetic letters. You can imagine how long it would take to decode that many Cs, Gs, As, and Ts. But there are shortcuts.

Outside the cell's nucleus, but inside the cell's membrane, in a gooey liquid called cytoplasm, you'll find mitochondria. Mitochondria are the cell's power plants. Their job is to make energy. Cells that require a lot of energy, such as brain and muscle cells, can contain as many as a thousand mitochondria—and each of those mitochondria contains a tiny piece of DNA. Mitochondrial DNA (mtDNA) is plentiful, which makes it easier to extract. And mtDNA is a short strand, which makes it faster to decode. But that's not all.

Unlike nuclear DNA, which comes from both parents, mtDNA is inherited only from the mother. Both types of DNA are subject to the occasional random mutation, but the cell isn't as vigilant about ferreting out mutations and correcting them in the mitochondria as it is in the nucleus. Twenty times as many mutations are passed down to subsequent generations in mtDNA as are passed down in nuclear DNA. By tracking and timing mutation rates, scientists are able to use DNA as a molecular clock. Too few mutations in a population, and everyone's DNA looks the same. It's those forks in the DNA road that mark time. With the mitochondrial clock ticking 20 times faster, it makes a good measure for human prehistory.

Much of animal behavior is genetically programmed, so why not language? And if there is a genetic basis for language, there should be a marker imbedded in the human genetic material—some change that separates the "before" from the "after." Sifting through tens of thousands of genes for a single mutation within the full set of human chromosomes is like looking for a needle in a haystack.

The task seemed insurmountable until British geneticist Jane Hurst stumbled across a family in London with severe speech problems. In the last three generations, 15 of 37 family members were affected by this genetic speech disability that prevented them from being able to move their tongue and lips to form words. A team of geneticists compared the genetic material—the 23 pairs of chromosomes of those family members who could speak to the 23 pairs of chromosomes of those who couldn't. They narrowed the mutation's location down to somewhere on chromosome 7. The team still faced a search that would be like looking for a needle in a haystack, but it would be a smaller haystack.

A breakthrough occurred when the team discovered a young boy with a similar speech problem as the British family's. The boy's chromosome 7, however, had a clearly visible break in it, making the defect, and therefore the speech gene, easy to pinpoint. Scientists named this gene associated with speech FOXP2.

Who better to trace the origins of FOXP2 than Svante Pääbo, at the Max Planck Institute for Evolutionary Anthropology in Germany. One of *Time* magazine's most influential people and the founder of paleogenetics (the study of DNA in ancient populations) Pääbo once said in an interview, "I'm driven by curiosity. I'm driven by exactly the same thing that makes an archaeologist go to Africa to look for bones of our ancestors."

Pääbo searched for the first sign of FOXP2 in DNA. Peering through owlish glasses, he found FOXP2 present in mice, which means the gene is a very old one, dating back to when humans and mice shared a common ancestor some 70 million years ago. Pääbo compared FOXP2 in mice to FOXP2 in humans and found only three differences. FOXP2 has undergone only three updates in 70 million years.

Humans and chimps haven't shared a common ancestor for 5 million years. So when in the last 5 million years did FOXP2 undergo that third change that opened the door for language? By comparing FOXP2 in different populations around the world, Pääbo was able to make a rough estimate. He estimated that this mutation, this last step in attaining all the necessary parts for speech, occurred within the last 200,000 years.

❖ ❖ ❖

After all this study, after all these deductions among all these disciplines, what did Alan Walker conclude about the 1.6-million-year-old Turkana Boy's speaking abilities? He decided that Pääbo and his colleagues were right about Turkana Boy, "[T]he boy could not talk and he could not think as we do. For all his human physique and physiology, the boy was still an animal—a clever one, a large one, a successful one—but an animal nonetheless."

For Walker this was a difficult admission. During the excavation and his lengthy study of Turkana Boy, Walker had grown attached to those old bones. Walker said that in the end, when he looked long and hard at Turkana Boy, what he saw looking back was "that deadly unknowing I have seen in a lion's blank yellow eyes. He may have been our ancestor, but there was no human consciousness within that human body. He was not one of us."

Further reading on Turkana Boy

Lynch, John, and Louise Barrett. *Walking with Cavemen: Eye-to-Eye with Your Ancestors.* New York: DK Publishing, 2003.

Walker, Alan, and Pat Shipman. *The Wisdom of the Bones: In Search of Human Origins.* New York: Knopf, 1996.

Websites

Hall of Human Origins/American Museum of Natural History
http://www.amnh.org/exhibitions/permanent/humanorigins/history/turkana.php
This site explores human fossil history. (Note: AMNH lists Turkana Boy's age as 8, not 9.)

KFRP Koobi Fora Research Project Lake Turkana
http://www.kfrp.com
Koobi Fora Research Project conducts research in the Turkana Basin.

Source notes (See Bibliography on p. 178 for full citations.)

"Keep them safe for me. . . ." *Origins Reconsidered: In Search of What Makes Us Human,* p. 8.

"OK, Walker. Let's see . . ." *Origins Reconsidered,* p. 25.

"We've found more bone. . . ." *Ancestral Passion: The Leakey Family and the Quest for Humankind's Beginning,* p. 536.

"to where Kamoya was sitting . . ." *Origins Reconsidered,* p. 40.

"like a demented grasshopper . . ." *The Wisdom of the Bones,* p. 16.

"But you can't understand them!" *The Wisdom of the Bones,* p. 22.

"Walker, if there's nothing more . . ." *The Wisdom of the Bones,* p. 17.

"Listen for the ping. . . ." *The Hominid Gang,* p. 238

"I want, I want . . ." *The Hominid Gang,* p. 238.

"The gluing team got smart . . ." *Origins Reconsidered,* p. 45.

"This is the first clavicle . . ." *Ancestral Passion,* p. 528.

"Give me your finger . . ." *The Wisdom of the Bones,* p. 22.

"the region of the brain . . ." *The Wisdom of the Bones,* p. 22.

"The boy could talk. . . ." *The Wisdom of the Bones,* p. 22.

"Kanzi would just be around . . ." Hamilton, Joy. "Exploring Language: A
    Voluble Visit with Two Talking Apes." NPR, January 7, 2007.

"Humans can fly . . ." Johnson, George. "Chimp Talk Debate: Is It Really
    Language?" *New York Times,* June 6, 1995, section C, page 1.

"No chimpanzee has learned . . ." Hart, Steven. *The Animal
    Communication Project,* 2007. http://acp.eugraph.com/apes/index.html

"I'm driven by curiosity. . . ." Olsen, Steve. "Neanderthal Man."
    Smithsonian magazine, October 2006.
    http://www.smithsonianmag.com/science-nature/neanderthal.html

"the boy could not talk . . ." *The Wisdom of the Bones,* p. 235.

"that deadly unknowing . . ." *The Wisdom of the Bones,* p. 235.

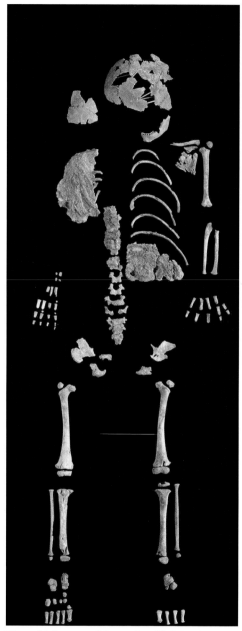

The skeleton of Lapedo Child whose robust lower limbs kicked off the hybrid debate.

Lapedo Child
Discovery

24,500 years ago . . .

They dressed the child's lifeless body in a headdress decorated with four deer teeth, one for each year of his short life, and his well-worn seashell pendant.

One last look, one last chance to say good-bye, and then they wrapped him in a shroud made from animal skin. The hide hugged him so snugly that it pushed the tops of his feet down, forcing his toes to point. Ocher, the red earth they had gathered and ground into a powder, stained their fingers crimson as they sprinkled it over the hide. They spread more and more, until the hide looked as if it had been soaked in blood.

They dug a shallow grave near the back wall of a deserted wolf den. In the bottom of the pit, they laid a single Scotch pine branch. When they set the branch on fire, smoke billowed from the pit and collected in the hollow under the overhang until it overflowed and spilled into the valley. After the last of the embers turned to charcoal, they placed the child's wrapped body on top of the cold fire and left him on his back, slightly tilted toward the rear wall of the rock shelter.

Would he need food where he was going? Would the spirits? As an offering they placed a rabbit on the child's legs and the best cuts from a red deer by his head and feet.

They loved him in life. They loved him still.

November 1998

What subject would make a great college term paper? If you were a college student who lived in a small Portuguese village near the Lapedo Valley, then prehistoric rock-wall paintings might come to mind. That's the topic Pedro Ferreira chose. He knew of a small ravine near his village that was a promising location for rock art. The ravine was hidden in a tumble of reeds, bushes, and Scotch pine. A road had been started and then abandoned, with construction debris left behind.

The ravine was no more than a mile long and not much wider than a stone toss. Archaeologists had found prehistoric drawings on nearby cliff walls. Ferreira thought that if they hadn't discovered this ravine, then he might be the first to search it for rock art.

Ferreira walked the length of the north side. The gray limestone cliff wall above his head curled out, folded back in, and curled out again. It looked as if he were walking alongside the tail of a giant dragon that had nestled in among the bushes. Ferreira examined the limestone folds inch by inch. Under an overhang he noticed an out-of-place color on the limestone—a deep red. He looked closer. There were three part-human, part-animal figures. Rock art. Ferreira had discovered his term paper.

When word of the discovery reached João Zilhão, the director of Portugal's National Museum of Archaeology, he dispatched two field assistants to authenticate the rock art. Ferreira led the field-workers to the site, where they immediately recognized the small red figures as old and man-made. They guessed the figures were drawn during the Copper Age, between 5,000 and 6,000 years ago. What else might they find?

They stood in the shelter of the overhang and studied the

opposite side of the ravine. Their years of working on archaeological projects had taught them to recognize promising prehistoric occupation sites. Above the scrub treetops, they noticed a long limestone lip jutting into the canyon like a giant rock awning. It was exactly the type of rock formation that prehistoric humans used for shelter. Zilhão's assistants crossed the ravine to check it out.

The long horizontal crevices in the limestone were packed with dirt that had settled there over the millennia. The field-workers noticed black flecks of charcoal in the sediments—signs of ancient campfires. People had lived here and left behind their litter—bones and stone tools were everywhere.

The field-workers circled an old tractor hood, squatted, and crept into a small cavelike hollow at the base of the cliff wall. They noticed an area of loose dirt. An animal burrow? They knew that when an animal digs its burrow and scuffs dirt toward the surface, it often kicks up archaeological remains along with the dirt. What had this animal dug up? With care, the workers poked at the loose dirt with trowels and their fingers. They found bones. *Could these be human bones?* they wondered. After gently reburying the bones, they took careful note of the exact location and then hurried off to call João Zilhão.

❖ ❖ ❖

The following Sunday João Zilhão and Cidália Duarte picked their way through the construction debris that littered the ravine. They stepped around the shell of an abandoned trailer, over a concrete drainpipe, and past the rusting tractor hood. Hardly Paleolithic remains. Earthmoving equipment had stamped a crosshatched pattern in the earth. Someone

This is the rock shelter in Lapedo Valley that archaeologists call Lagar Velho. The limestone overhang bulges out over the burial place of Lapedo Child.

had begun the grading for a dirt road. By the looks of the plant regrowth, they had given up on the project a few years before.

Zilhão had invited Duarte to join him because of her specialty. She was an expert in how bodies were buried and preserved. If the bones Zilhão's assistants found were human, Duarte would be the perfect person to excavate them.

From where they stood, northeast of the rock shelter, the scientists noted with growing excitement the limestone layers of alternating overhangs and cavities—so many lovely nooks and crannies to trap ancient sediments. But when they reached the rock shelter, what they saw made their hearts sink. White scratch marks from the teeth of a Caterpillar's digging claw gouged the back wall. Neither of the scientists wanted to think about what that could mean in terms of destruction.

They split up. Zilhão surveyed the site while Duarte inspected the bones.

It didn't take long for either expert to find clues. Zilhão found Paleolithic tools. Everywhere he looked, his trained eye picked up evidence that prehistoric people had spent time here—made their tools here, cooked here, maybe even lived here.

At the base of the limestone wall, tucked into the hollow, Duarte found the bones that the field-workers had discovered. She knew they were arm bones. "Ooh—this is human! This is a kid!" she said.

Zilhão looked down from the overhang to where Duarte kneeled by the bones. Then he looked up the scarred face of the cliff. Every foot of the wall represented passage of time. Archaeologists know that the deeper you dig, the farther you go back in time. Sometimes an inch can traverse hundreds, even thousands, of years. Since the child's bones were embedded in undisturbed sediments so many feet below the tools, the child had died thousands of years before the tools had been crafted.

Zilhão climbed down to watch Duarte carefully brushing sediment aside. She showed the arm bones to Zilhão. He noticed the odd color of the bones. This wasn't from natural aging; it was something he had seen many times before. The bones were stained with red ocher, a pigment often used in ancient burial rituals. Stunned, they both stared at the bones. These were the bones of a Paleolithic child burial. This was the first Paleolithic burial ever discovered in the Iberian Peninsula.

Later Zilhão told reporters, "I immediately recognized something big was here. The question was whether the bulldozing had completely destroyed the burial, and all that we had to do was collect fragments, or if something was still there intact."

On their ride back to Lisbon, they barely noticed the 87 miles zip by. Did they dare believe this discovery was what they thought it was? Could this really be a Paleolithic human ritual burial? Zilhão pulled to the side of the road and stopped the car. The scientists jumped out, opened the bags holding the bones, and took another look. Yes, red ocher, no question. They climbed back into the car but were only a few miles farther along when the questions started all over again.

How much damage had the earthmoving equipment done? What about the burrowing animal? What if the rest of the child's bones had been scattered, crushed, chewed, or destroyed? And yet—they couldn't contain that rush of hope that the child was in situ, in its original position—what if *most* of the site had never been disturbed? Zilhão stopped the car again. They hopped out and reopened the bags. Still there . . . still red. They jumped back into the car.

What should they name the site? Maybe Lagar Velho, meaning "old olive press," after the beat-up olive press at the entrance of the ravine? They decided that they had to keep Lagar Velho secret, at least until they knew more. Yes, secret, top secret. Still not quite believing it was real, they stopped the car, jumped out, and opened the bags yet again. . . .

The work week dragged on for Zilhão and Duarte. Neither one spoke of the child, the red bones, or Lagar Velho. When they passed one another in the museum hallways, they didn't speak of the find. The site was unprotected. They wouldn't put it at risk by revealing anything before they started a salvage operation. Even then, secrecy would be important. Opportunists, souvenir hunters, or even those who are merely curious can damage a site.

All week Zilhão and Duarte were plagued with worry. What if those arm bones were all that was left? The sheer number of tools, bones, and charcoal told Zilhão that this was an important occupation site. Just how much remained?

Zilhão planned a two-day expedition to Lagar Velho for that weekend in order to begin his work. He planned to profile the site and record the positions of ancient remnants. Duarte would work in the hollow with one other trusted archaeologist. On the drive to Lapedo Valley, the three went over their strategies for attacking the site.

Zilhão mapped the site by stringing a grid. He stretched and secured lengths of string until the ground was blanketed by a giant string graph. He repeated the process over a spot they called the hanging remnant. And again over the place Duarte believed the skeleton would be found, which they called the bone level. After each square of the stringed grids had been labeled for mapping finds, Zilhão turned his attention to what lay inside those squares.

Zilhão was particularly interested in the coprolites, or fossilized feces. Coprolites would provide the hard evidence of which animals had been in the area thousands of years before. Zilhão found fossilized droppings from horse and deer, and with growing worry, he found coprolites from a number of gnawing animals—animals that like to chew on bones.

Zilhão found fossilized bones and horse teeth. He found charcoal and stone tools. Meticulously, he recorded each fossil and artifact in his field notebook.

While Zilhão was striking it rich in the hanging remnant,

Duarte wasn't having much luck in the bone level. For two days she sifted through sediments. "By Sunday evening we were really upset, because all we could find were bits and pieces, fragments of bone, and they didn't even have this reddish color," she said.

Too soon it was time to pack up and get back to Lisbon for work on Monday. The previous Sunday the car had practically rocked with their excitement—tonight's ride home would probably be pretty subdued. With her spirits as dim as the failing light, she began to clean up the site. She used a paintbrush to sweep loose surface dirt from her work area into plastic bags to take back to the lab. Her brushstrokes lacked her usual enthusiasm. It was hard not to be discouraged after a week of high hopes.

At first the red under the loose sediment didn't register, but her training automatically stilled her hand. Gently she brushed a bit more, and more and more, until she had exposed a deep red stain the size of a young child.

❖ ❖ ❖

Secrecy was now more important than ever. The child's skeleton lay just below the surface. Anything could happen to it. Zilhão's team even grew suspicious of the Boy Scouts. A troop hiking by earlier had shown a little too much interest for comfort. While Duarte camouflaged the area, Zilhão arranged for a guard. Before leaving the site, they pulled the rusted tractor hood over the burial site as much to protect it from the forecasted rain as to disguise it.

Late that night, back in Lisbon, Zilhão sent an email to an expert who worked at Washington University in the United States. Erik Trinkaus had excavated many Paleolithic human

Cidália Duarte uncovers Lapedo Child's remains, which are tucked under the overhang and are close to the rock wall. Red ochre stains were Duarte's first clue that a burial might be found here.

burials and was respected for his lab work analyzing Paleolithic human remains. He was a leading scholar in human origins, and the perfect person to consult on Lapedo Child.

> *From: João Zilhão*
> *To: Erik Trinkaus*
> *Cc: Cidália Duarte*
> *Sent: 13 de Dezembro de 1998 23:46*
> *Subject: An early Upper Paleolithic child burial*
> *in Portugal*
> *Dear Erik,*
> *. . . I was called to go see a new site—a large rock*

shelter where the owner had scraped the upper
part of the fill in order to make a path large
enough for his tractor. . . .
I went there with Cidália and . . . we confirmed
that a few bones . . . were human. I noticed that
they seemed quite reddish by comparison with the
non-human bones in the site. Besides they
represented the forearm and the hand of a young
child. All of this suggested that we might be
dealing with an ochered burial. So, this weekend,
we went back to make sure. The results are the
following:
1) There is indeed a burial. It is a miracle that it
was not destroyed by the [C]aterpillar that
terraced the site. . . . The skull bones are heavily
ochered and the sediment around was ochre
stained. . . . The bones belong to a child, probably
a 4–5 year old boy. The chin is there, so it is a
modern human.
2) . . . The important thing in regard to the burial
is that [it is from] 21,000 BP [before present]. . . .
the first Paleolithic burial ever excavated in
Iberia.
. . . We had to stop when the night fell a few hours
ago. A collaborator will look after the site
permanently for the rest of the week and we will
go back next Friday night prepared to spend as
much time as needed until we finish the
excavation of the burial. . . . Cidália is doing the
excavation, very carefully, mapping and drawing
everything and saving the totality of the sediment
for future screening. If you have any suggestions

on how to proceed, please let us know. Naturally,
we are counting on your guidance for the study of
the human remains.

Best,
João Zilhão

❖ ❖ ❖

With a mouse click, Zilhão revealed their discovery to one of
the select few he would confide in over the next few days. He
and Duarte maintained a code of silence around others, but
in secret they prepared to dig in earnest. Duarte put in for
vacation time, and Zilhão simply disappeared from his director's duties. "I just went away without telling anybody," he
said, "so as not to run the risk of a leak."

❖ ❖ ❖

For three solid weeks rain chilled them to the bone—cold, raw,
and wet, day after day after day. Zilhão, Duarte, and the small
team they had put together worked despite the discomfort, in-
creasingly alarmed by what exposure to the air was doing to
the burial site. The dampness made it impossible to apply the
chemicals necessary to preserve and strengthen the child's
bones. The bones weakened, and the ocher color paled. The
condition of the site deteriorated a little more each day.

Excavation isn't a job that can be hurried, and so the
team fought the weather's attack on the site with long hours,
eking out every moment of daylight, working from dawn to
dusk without a day's rest.

Layer by paper-thin layer, the skeleton emerged from the

Lapedo Child's leg and foot bones are shown here in situ.

Archaeologists sketch their discoveries on graph paper to render details to scale. Here Duarte drew Lapedo Child's leg bones as they appear in situ (see above photograph).

sediment as Duarte cleared away the dirt—the shoulder, the ribs, the legs, the feet. Duarte recorded each bone's X, Y, and Z coordinates in her field notebook. The work was tedious, requiring Duarte's full attention. Tiny plant roots had wormed their way through the spongy bones. Freeing the bones without damaging them was delicate work.

They took hundreds of pictures, in black and white, in color, on slides, and on videotape—recording every bone's position relative to the site and to one another.

Most of the cranium was gone, shattered by a swipe of the Cat, the pieces pushed away and mixed into the dirt. Later, when the dirt was sieved, they would find 160 fragments, nearly 80 percent of the skull. The child's right arm up to the shoulder had also been badly damaged. The rest of the body, buried just three-quarters of an inch deeper, had escaped the rumbling earthmover.

Every night, after they tidied up the site, collected their tools, and stretched their weary muscles, Duarte and her coworkers hid the child under the old tractor hood. Every rainy morning they uncovered him again. Christmas Eve was the only concession they allowed themselves, leaving the site a bit earlier than usual to spend time with their families.

Zilhão and Trinkaus exchanged emails almost nightly, Zilhão attaching digital pictures to show their daily progress. Trinkaus would have hopped the first flight to Portugal if it weren't for his fall semester teaching duties. His plan was to join the team shortly after New Year's. For now pictures and emails would have to satisfy his growing curiosity about this unusual skeleton.

Trinkaus wasn't the only one having a hard time containing his curiosity. In the village, gossip traveled quickly. The locals weren't fooled by all the cloak-and-dagger behavior.

They knew something was going on in the ravine and were determined to find out what. At first one or two townsfolk followed the archaeologists and snooped around the site. Soon groups came to watch the team work. With the news spreading so quickly, the scientists were forced to hire around-the-clock security. Lapedo Child was too valuable to have nothing more than an old tractor hood for protection.

On Christmas Day Duarte was alone at the site with the child. "I wasn't going to leave it there all exposed," she said. But it wasn't only the child's welfare that worried Duarte. Things were about to change, and she knew it. While she worked, Duarte couldn't stop thinking about the story Portuguese public television would be broadcasting later that day. In honor of the holiday, they had named the segment "Christmas Child." By the end of the day, the whole world would know about Lapedo Child. Soon visitors would swarm the site. Tours would be scheduled to control the crowds. Security would be beefed up. This would be Duarte's last chance to be alone with the child.

It was good to have the peace and quiet because the day's work was particularly finicky. Duarte was laying bare the delicate rib cage. She filled a syringe with acetone, the same chemical used in nail polish remover. Acetone dissolves caked-on dirt in the same way it dissolves nail polish, and yet it evaporates so quickly it doesn't penetrate the bone.

Kneeling beside Lapedo Child, Duarte pushed the plunger on the syringe and squirted acetone between two ribs. As soon as the acetone dried, she used a soft paintbrush to sweep the loosened dirt from between the bones. Then, while looking through a magnifying glass to be sure she didn't damage the rib, she gently prodded the more stubborn bits of dirt with a wooden toothpick.

Excavation exposes Lapedo Child's ribcage and spinal column,
which is stained from red ochre pigment.

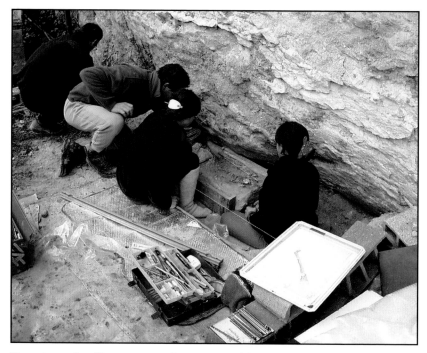

Duarte and colleagues perform an en bloc removal of Lapedo Child's delicate ribcage. Back in the lab Duarte will be able to remove the bones from the block with minimal damage.

When her legs began to tingle, Duarte switched her position, sometimes lying down alongside the child to get a better angle. After enough loose dirt had accumulated, she cleared it out of the way with a plastic spoon and shoveled it into a plastic bag to examine later in the laboratory. Duarte was so focused she barely noticed the rain, the numbing cold, or the long hours that passed.

❖ ❖ ❖

On January 3, 1999, Duarte led her team through the final

stage of the child's salvage operation. They cut a block around the delicate rib cage, digging well below the bone level to make sure the dirt supporting the bones remained undisturbed. A box was built and assembled around the block of soil-packed bones so that the block could be lifted intact with no trauma to the bones. Archaeologists call this an en bloc removal.

Duarte returned to the National Museum in Lisbon with this last part of Lapedo Child's skeleton. Trinkaus and Zilhão, who had already begun cleaning, measuring, and reassembling the child's bones, were only now getting an inkling as to how controversial those bones might be. This 4-year-old Lapedo Child might just solve one of the biggest mysteries in anthropology.

Deductions
Lapedo Child

A major discovery like Lapedo Child brings scholars out of the woodwork. Researchers scramble to put together proposals in hopes of getting an opportunity to use the ancient remains to expand their own studies. There are sciences involved that most people have never even heard of, many beginning with the Greek prefixes "paleo" and "archaeo," meaning old, ancient, prehistoric, early, or primitive—and Lapedo Child was all of that.

It takes scientists from every discipline to develop a full picture of our prehistoric past. When they first arrive at a site, scientists have no idea what they are going to find. Will it be an isolated find? Or will the entire area be an archaeological treasure trove, with finds marking the millennia? Will the site produce one academic paper or be the subject of a lifetime of work? Here are just a few of the discoveries Lapedo Child led them to.

Paleopathologists study skeletons for evidence of ancient diseases

When a child as young as Turkana Boy or Lapedo Child dies, the first question is often why. Lapedo Child's bones were typical of a healthy young boy. His hip, knee, foot, and leg bones all grew as expected, indicating that the boy had walked, run, and jumped like any other 4-year-old. If his movements had been impaired or his lower limbs unable to hold up his weight, then his bones would have grown abnormally. His had not.

There were a few marks on Lapedo Child's bones that indicated he had fallen or been struck hard enough to cause some serious bruises, but not hard enough to break a bone. One blow was to the lower left side of his face, and the other to his left forearm. Neither injury would have bothered him for long, nor were they serious enough to have killed him.

A paleopathologist examined Lapedo Child's teeth, looking for signs of illness. Defects in the tooth enamel were visible to the naked eye, but just barely. From the size of the defects, scientists deduced that the boy was sick twice for a period of 18 to 20 days each time. Famine can prevent tooth enamel from growing normally, but it's unlikely that Lapedo Child experienced times when food was impossible to find. That kind of malnutrition would have caused larger defects. The most likely cause of the defects was a childhood fever.

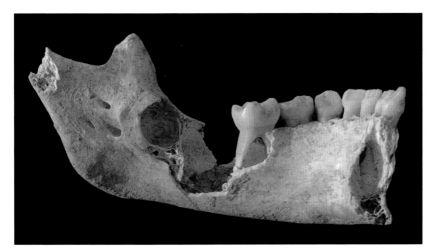

Lapedo Child's mandible (with teeth still in place) illustrates a snowplow-shaped jaw, not typical of modern humans.

A paleopathologist measured the positions of the defects on the teeth and compared the teeth to tooth growth charts. Unlike Turkana Boy where scientists needed to develop a dental model for *Homo erectus* before calculating his age, scientists working on the Lapedo Child were able to compare his teeth to modern humans' teeth. Lapedo Child had just turned 4 when the first fever struck. The second illness occurred about two and a half months later, just two months before he died.

Other than these bumps, bruises, and two childhood illnesses, the skeleton showed a healthy individual. Lapedo Child's cause of death remained a mystery.

Geoarchaeologists study soil and the landscape for evidence of human occupation

The geoarchaeologists were most interested in the area above Lapedo Child, the hanging remnant. It ran along the entire length of the back wall of the shelter. This opening in the overhang, located about two feet off the ground, was full of loosely packed sand that had accumulated during the last ice age. The geoarchaeologists combed through areas where the elevation was only inches higher than the level in which Lapedo Child had been buried, and yet those inches represented thousands of years.

Archaeologists often have to remove a lot of dirt before they get down to the level where humans once lived. At Lagar Velho two test pits were excavated, exposing a large open area that dated back 22,500 years. In this occupation level, the geoarchaeologists found two hearths about 10 feet apart, surrounded by burned bones. From the clusters of animal bones and the flakes of stone (a by-product of stone toolmaking), a picture emerged of how the occupation level was used.

Around one of the hearths, the geoarchaeologists found several groups of scattered stone chips. The chips showed where prehistoric toolmakers had sat and made tools with a rounded hammering stone scientists call a cobble and flint blocks. Toolmakers whacked at a block of flint with a fist-sized cobble. It took skill to know precisely where and at what angle to strike the flint so that it flaked into sharp cutting edges.

The area between the two hearths was thick with animal bones, indicating that this was where hunted animals had been skinned and butchered. In this spot prehistoric residents had butchered 20 different kinds of animals. Their favorite seemed to have been red deer.

West of the tenth row of the hanging remnant's stringed grid, the sediment grew thick with ancient debris. From just a few test pits, the scholars bagged and tagged 32,000 animal bones, 6,000 stone artifacts, and thousands of charcoal fragments.

At first the geoarchaeologists thought so much debris meant that the shelter had been occupied by a very large group of people for a very long period of time. Then they noticed that the ground gently sloped toward the back wall. They realized that over time the debris must have slid down the incline and accumulated against the back wall, making it appear as if the shelter had been more densely populated than it actually was. A sample taken farther away from the wall would probably tell a different story. It might look as if hardly anyone lived there at all.

The people who used this site for cooking, toolmaking, and meat processing went about their days unaware that a child had been buried thousands of years before, and that his skeleton lay beneath them.

Paleobotanists study vegetation from the past to reconstruct ancient environments

The paleobotanists dug under Lapedo Child's burial, sampling sediments for pollen in four layers that dated between 25,000 and 27,000 years ago. Their mission was to paint a picture of the vegetation in the area all those thousands of years ago. They would reconstruct the growth in the area by comparing concentrations of pollen. Did wild rose grow then, as it does today? And if so, how many wild rosebushes were there compared to, say, brambles?

Preparing sediment samples to calculate pollen concentrations is no easy task. It's a tedious process that has many steps. First the paleobotanists sieve the sediment through a mesh, using water to keep fine material (like pollen) from billowing into the air. Then they bathe the sediments in hydrochloric acid at room temperature until the bubbling stops. They follow that with a bath of hydrofluoric acid, allowing the sediment to soak for several days. The baths continue with five-minute dunks in various chemicals that are heated to temperatures high enough to boil water. When the baths are done, the scholars agitate the mixture for 20 minutes before centrifuging it—2,000 rotations in 10 minutes. The agitation and rotation steps are repeated three times. Then the material is filtered through a fine powder which traps the pollen. The whole lot is immersed in acid until the powder dissolves. Finally the samples are dehydrated with alcohol and mounted onto slides with silicone oil.

After all that work, the paleobotanists studying Lapedo Child discovered that the pollen preservation was too poor to reconstruct the ancient environment. Fragile pollens had disintegrated and disappeared from the samples. Hardy pollens, such as Scotch pine, dominated their slides. The ratios were completely out of whack. What they were looking at through their microscopes was solely dependent on whether the plants had flimsy pollen or not, and not on how plentiful the plant had been at the time.

Discouraged, the scholars turned their attention to the charcoal in the hearths. What kind of wood did these prehistoric occupants use to fuel their fires? The paleobotanists collected hundreds of fragments, broke them by hand, and took a close look through reflected-light optical microscopes. Those early fire builders had clear favorites. They liked Scotch pine, Scotch broom, and heath, but they also burned elm, ivy, and oak. But knowing what the ancients burned didn't give the scientists an accurate picture of the total environment; it only showed what prehistoric people chose to throw on the fire.

What plants did the ancients choose for their burial rituals? The charcoal fragments from Lapedo Child's burial pit turned to powder when the scholars tried to break them into pieces for microscopic examination. Despite the charcoal's fragility, though, the paleobotanists were able to identify the wood beneath the child as a single branch of Scotch pine.

Archaeozoologists study animal remains to find evidence about ancient human/animal relationships

The archaeozoologists went bone collecting. They examined the grid squares in the overhang. They worked the site, dry-sieving and sometimes water-sieving sediment from the squares through a mesh just like the Hominid Gang had sifted for Turkana Boy's bones. Back at a laboratory in Lisbon, they compared the bones they found to a reference bone collection. They were able to identify the animals by matching the shape and size of the bones taken from the site to the bones in the collection.

The archaeozoologists found bones from a variety of mammals (including horses, ibex, red deer, and wild boars), birds (including common buzzards and choughs, a kind of raven), amphibians, and rodents (including rabbits, squirrels, and water voles).

They then examined the bones to see if they could answer the question, What were so many animal bones doing there? The archaeozoologists found four clues: bites, pits, cuts, and burns.

Some of the bones had gnaw marks on them, indicating that scavengers were responsible for little piles here and there. A number of teeth showed pitting from stomach acid. Those teeth had been digested. Carnivores and birds of prey had deposited these at the site in their feces.

In some areas of the site, the archaeozoologists found bones with cut marks on them, evidence that humans had butchered animals there. They also found many burned bones, evidence of cooking. When the archaeozoologists picked through the hearths, they found burned rabbit feet, evidence that the rabbits were most likely roasted whole. A picture of how humans had used the site was emerging.

The surfaces of the bones showed wear consistent with exposure to the elements prior to being buried under layers of sediment. This led the archaeozoologists to believe that thousands of years ago the hanging remnant was open to the air, not protected.

The types of animal bones found gave archaeozoologists a clue as to what the surrounding area may have looked like. Red deer and squirrels are forest animals. Choughs breed in mountains with steep cliffs and ravines. Water voles burrow alongside rivers in wet soil. Bone by bone, a picture of the ancient environment developed.

❖ ❖ ❖

Of the thousands upon thousands of finds at Lagar Velho, six have special significance—four deer teeth and two periwinkle shells. Only one was found in situ—Duarte found a periwinkle shell resting on Lapedo Child's left shoulder. The rest had been scattered by the earthmoving equipment.

Working under a microscope, the archaeozoologists used wooden toothpicks to gently scrape away the red ocher that coated the deer teeth and periwinkle shells. All the scrapings were saved for future analysis. Each tooth and shell was cleaned with distilled water and a soft paintbrush. The scientists discovered that two of the teeth came from stags and two from does.

While examining these teeth, the archaeologists noticed that they had piercings and the hole sizes varied. The techniques used to make the holes differed, too. The ancient crafters had used very small strokes as they scraped through the tooth with a sharp gouging tool. As a finishing touch, they had rotated a pointed tool in a drill-like motion through the hole. The workmanship on the stag teeth was excellent, but someone less experienced had pierced the doe teeth. The scientists determined that at least two, probably three, different people had pierced the teeth.

The crafter who pierced the stag teeth had used weather-worn teeth, perhaps collected and saved for a project like this one. Thread, now long gone, had been strung through the holes, cutting deeply into only one side of the teeth. This led the archaeozoologists to believe that a thread had been tied snugly to the side. They hadn't swung freely. The teeth had not been worn as pendants. The way the thread had cut into the teeth and the fact that the teeth were found near the shattered skull indicated that the teeth may have decorated a headdress.

Curious about the crafter's technique, the scientists tried their hand at piercing deer teeth. It took them two hours to pierce just one tooth. Piercing periwinkle shells was even more difficult. They broke more than half of the shells. They concluded that the crafters who had made the seashell pendants had understood the periwinkle's architecture perfectly in order to puncture it without breaking it. The skill of piercing shells is in locating the best place on the shell wall and applying just the right amount of pressure.

The circumferences of the shell piercings were enlarged from wear. The periwinkle pendants, like the deer-toothed headdress, hadn't been made just for the burial. Someone had worn them. All six items had been used for personal adornment. The ancients at Lagar Velho had cherished something for its beauty or its meaning rather than just its function.

❖ ❖ ❖

All the scientific disciplines were intrigued by the deep red stain from the ocher. Ocher had penetrated the top and the bottom of the bones, leading the scientists to believe that the child's body had been wrapped in an ocher-painted shroud of animal skin. Over the millennia the animal skin decayed, as did the child's flesh. With the barriers gone, ocher sank into the bones and into the sediment around them. A cocoonlike hide wrap would also explain why the child's feet had been forced to point downward.

Shown here are the six ornaments found with Lapedo Child. There are four red deer canines (above) and two periwinkle shells (below) all stained with the same red ochre pigment that colored Lapedo Child's remains.

Not only were the child's bones saturated with pigment, but the rabbit bones found between the child's legs were as well. The scientists believed that the rabbit carcass could have been buried with the child as a food offering.

And then there's the evidence no scientist expects to find

Everything about Lapedo Child indicated that he was a modern human. The chin was modern. The red ocher burial was a common modern human ritual. Also, the scientists had dated the Scotch pine in the grave pit to the time when moderns had inhabited Portugal. Scholars believed that Neandertals, an ancient human species that lived primarily in Europe and Southwest Asia, had disappeared from Europe 29,000 years ago. Duarte was working a level not quite 25,000 years old. So she assumed that she was unearthing a modern human child. From the sturdiness of the arm and leg bones, Duarte guessed a boy child. But in the lab, the bone measurements weren't adding up.

The bones presented a confusing jumble of modern human and Neandertal features. The child had a chin and small teeth like a modern human, but below those small teeth and behind the pointed chin, the jaw swept back like a Neandertal's. The shape of the skull was modern, but the lower part was pitted, a genetic trait found only in Neandertals. Who was this child? Trinkaus measured and measured again.

Years before, Trinkaus had published a paper on limb evolution. He created and maintained an extensive database of arm and leg bone measurements, which he'd compiled for his research. He'd observed that people who live near the equator are taller than people who live near the poles. Turkana Boy's proximity to the equator was one reason he grew so tall. The farther you get from the equator, the shorter your tibia, or shinbone.

Neandertals were perfectly built for the ice age environment. Their limbs were what anthropologists call "robust"— powerfully built. Modern humans in Europe, on the other hand, had a tropical stature like Turkana Boy's.

When Trinkaus measured Lapedo Child's limbs and found them to be robust, he emailed Zilhão. "The end of last week I made some quick comparisons of the Lagar Velho leg bone proportions with some data that I have, and it comes out looking Neandertal!" Always cautious, as scholars tend to be, Trinkaus added, "unless I have made some silly mistake."

Zilhão and Duarte double-checked Trinkaus's measurements. Sure enough, there had been no silly mistake. Lapedo Child's limbs looked Neandertal. That and the snowplow-shaped jaw convinced them that the child was a hybrid of Neandertals and modern humans. "The kid surprised us," Trinkaus said. "The mosaic of anatomical features tells us that when Neandertals and modern humans met, they regularly interbred."

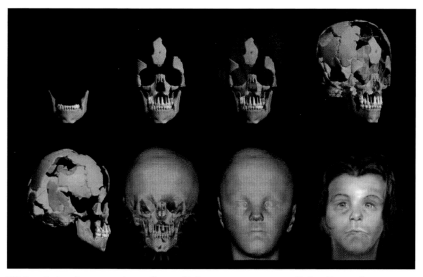

This virtual reconstruction of the appearance of the Lapedo Child's face is based on the techniques of forensic anthropology.

What probably didn't surprise Trinkaus was the reaction to his statement. The debate over Lapedo Child's ancestry that followed sunk to mudslinging levels. Unfortunately scholars couldn't turn to Lapedo Child's DNA, which they can extract from some Neandertal skeletons, for answers. The necessary collagen needed for a sample was gone from the child's bones. Scholars were left to duke it out, and they nearly did.

Debates
Lapedo Child

Scientists have been fighting about Neandertals ever since 1856, when the first Neandertal bones were discovered in the Neander Valley—or as the Germans call it, *Neander Tal*. The quarrymen who found the skeleton and thick skullcap, with its sloping forehead and brutish browridge, told their foreman they had discovered the skull of a beast. The foreman was sure it was the remains of an ancient cave bear. He brought the skeleton to a schoolteacher who decided that the remains most likely belonged to an ancestor to humans. But that didn't go over well at all. That thug? Human? Impossible.

The remains' thighbones were deformed, and scientists concluded that they were curved from childhood rickets. The fact that the thighbones were thicker than healthy human bones and not emaciated from malnutrition, which causes rickets, was conveniently overlooked.

No, not rickets, another set of scientists argued—the thighbones were curved from a life spent in the saddle. The bones weren't ancient, they claimed, but belonged to a Cossack soldier who had been wounded on his way to wage war with France. He must have crawled into the cave to die. No one bothered to ask where his armor, weapons, and clothing had gone.

The scientists had to stretch to find a human connection for the massive browridge. They claimed the brow had grown prominent from habitual frowning—probably from excessive flatulence brought on by the rickets. Yes, they decided, that must be it—a farting, wounded, Cossack soldier with rickets.

Then they found more skeletons.

How many farting, wounded, Cossack soldiers with rickets could there be? It took eight years for scientists to admit that this was no modern human with some bizarre affliction and finally assign a scientific name to the individuals with the brutish bones—*Homo neanderthalensis.*

But who was he, this Neandertal? Man or beast?

Scholars, who can never seem to agree on anything, concurred for once—this dim-witted, knuckle-dragging, grunting hulk was nothing like the noble, intelligent "we." At least they agreed on that one point until the late 1950s, when an archaeologist unearthed nine Neandertals buried in Shanidar Cave in Iraq. The Neandertals there had placed the body of an old man on a woven mat and buried him. Soil samples showed a large quantity of wildflower pollen. Neandertals weren't beasts, after all. They were flower children!

Once again debates raged over the nature of the Neandertal. One side claimed that no Neandertal would bring flowers to a funeral. The wind must have blown pollen into the grave. Or perhaps rodents had dragged the flowers in. Some said the only reason Neandertals buried their dead was because rotting corpses attract large carnivores—and because they stink.

Scientists also argued over where the Neandertal should sit on the evolutionary "bush." Is *Homo neanderthalensis* one of us—a direct ancestor? Or some evolutionary dead end—a twig that branched off before hominins were human?

The task of identifying the genes in Neandertal DNA fell to Svante Pääbo, the same genetic anthropologist who had worked on identifying the speech gene FOXP2. Pääbo could often be found in his lab wearing a Hawaiian shirt, clogs, and silly socks. While not exactly a fashion icon, he was a trailblazer in the analysis of Neandertal DNA. Pääbo believed Neandertal DNA would resolve some ancestry debates. By reassembling Neandertal DNA, Pääbo hoped to determine how Neandertals are related to humans living today and if they interbred with modern humans, as some say Lapedo Child suggests. If Neandertal and modern human populations interbred, the evidence should lie in the genetic instructions of people living today. But first Pääbo had to retrieve DNA— DNA that had survived tens of thousands of years.

After extracting the mtDNA from the upper right arm bone of a 42,000-year-old Neandertal fossil, Pääbo studied it and found those mtDNA sequences to be unlike mtDNA sequences found in people living today. Pääbo's mtDNA results favored the theory of little, if any, interbreeding between Neandertals and modern humans. But some scientists argued that because mtDNA strands are shorter than nuclear DNA strands, the information found in them isn't as complete.

Pääbo needed nuclear DNA from a Neandertal to create a complete picture. Finding a museum that would allow him to destroy Neandertal fossils by drilling holes in the rare and irreplaceable bones, grinding up the precious material, and then dissolving it in chemicals would prove to be a challenge. The carrot Pääbo dangled before the museum curators was the development of a new technique with the potential of recreating an entire DNA sequence. In essence he would end up with the blueprint for a Neandertal.

Pääbo planned to then compare Neandertal DNA to the DNA of present-day populations. Those comparisons could reveal genetic changes that would define where, when, and how hominins became humans. With those answers Pääbo might help settle one of the oldest debates in anthropology, *How* did modern humans disperse throughout the world?

Almost all scientists agree on one point. Human ancestors originated in Africa. After that it gets dicey. The debates are so heated that some scholars are no longer on speaking terms. At more than one conference, the "discussions" have nearly degenerated into fistfights. These conflicting theories are called the out-of-Africa model and the multiregional model.

The out-of-Africa model has modern humans evolving first in Africa and then spreading out all over the world, driving populations to extinction as they encountered them. The multiregional model has an *ancestor* of modern humans, perhaps someone like Turkana Boy, trekking out of Africa and spreading all over the world. Only then, after the dispersal, do modern humans evolve in different parts of the world.

Which model did Zilhão think Lapedo Child supported?

In an interview with the *London Observer,* Zilhão said, "There is an idea that modern humans emerged out of Africa like the chosen people. Their arrival is portrayed almost like a Biblical event, these golden ones replacing debased Europeans, the Neandertals. This is nonsense."

If the multiregional model explains modern human dispersal, then Neandertal genes should have survived in modern Europeans. Have they? In 2006 Pääbo began a two-year study, hoping to find out. Drilling into a Neandertal fossil found in Croatia, a bone specialist extracted a sample for Pääbo to study. Once the Neandertal DNA had been separated from bacteria and from the genetic material of people who had handled the fossil, Pääbo started reassembling the DNA. To date, Pääbo has found little evidence that suggests interbreeding.

But what about Lapedo Child's mixed Neandertal/modern human features? If he really was a descendant of these two very different cultures, then the two populations must have interbred at some point. Naturally, like all things Neandertal, scientists are divided on the issue of mating.

Trinkaus argued that Lapedo Child showed Neandertal features thousands of years after the Neandertals disappeared. For that to happen, the two populations must have mixed substantially.

Many scientists agree with Trinkaus. They believe the small Neandertal population was overwhelmed. After hundreds of generations of interbreeding, Neandertal features were watered down, until eventually they fizzled out.

A growing number of scientists disagree. They believe that Lapedo Child represents nothing more than a chunky modern human child. They point out that Pääbo's latest genetic research found no evidence that we carry Neandertal genes.

Then there are those who choose the middle of the road. They think that Neandertals and modern humans could have mated, but did so rarely—certainly not often enough to leave a stamp on the genetic code.

Neandertals make their first appearance in the fossil record some 230,000 years ago, and their last around 29,000 years ago. Scholars believe that modern humans infiltrated Spain nearly 40,000 years ago, spreading south 10,000 years later. So for several thousand years Neandertals and modern humans coexisted. They were neighbors. Yet none of the sites discovered so far contain remains from both. It appears as if the two populations kept their distance.

Eric Trinkaus was undaunted. He told one reporter, "They both would have been dirty and smelly by our standards. They would have been oblivious to the small anatomical differences, like certain details at the base of the Neanderthal skull. To each other, they would have both been people."

Yet Pääbo's research suggested Neandertals went extinct without contributing to our gene pool, making the premise that Lapedo Child was a hybrid look bleak. Other than a few features in a young child, whose body may simply have been built for the cold, the hard evidence is not there.

The debates over Lapedo Child's ancestry reopened one argument in particular. If Neandertal genes weren't diluted by extensive mating, how then do we explain their demise?

Scientists don't agree on the reason for Neandertal extinction any more than they do about anything else Neandertal. Why don't you live next door to a Neandertal? (Some argue that you do.) What happened to them? How did they die out?

Interbreeding isn't the only way to extinguish a population. If you've got an advantage, it's possible to outcompete a population—get the best hunting grounds, the best caves, the best stone for tools. Many scientists say that modern humans' advantage was language. They believe that while Neandertals have the identical FOXP2 gene as modern humans, the evidence suggests that they "spoke" with little more than grunts. Modern humans, on the other hand, spoke well enough to organize hunts, tell one another where the best root vegetables grew, pass information from one tribe or generation to the next—in other words, they could talk.

Other scientists blame Neandertal demise on tool technology. Neandertals didn't appear to have the imagination it takes to be innovative. Their tool design remained unchanged until long after modern humans appeared on the scene. Any 11th-hour changes in Neandertal toolmaking were "borrowed" from modern humans.

Not only were Neandertal tools *exactly* the same for thousands of years, Neandertals in France were flaking stone tools the same way as Neandertals in Russia. There were no regional differences in tools, as we see with humans today—for instance, in the fork versus chopsticks.

Meanwhile modern humans were not only discovering better tool design, such as a spear that could be thrown rather than thrust, but those clever fellows were also experimenting with new tool materials such as bone and antler.

It's hard to imagine robust, built-for-the-cold Neandertals edged off the glacier by our scrawny predecessors. But as scholars often say, Neandertals didn't have to fail—they just had to succeed less than their modern human neighbors. In *The Neandertal Enigma,* James Shreeve wrote that modern humans "only had to produce a few more babies every year than the beetle-browed others they occasionally met, and after a couple of thousand years, the job was done."

In anticipation of the publication of Pääbo's genetic research, the argument over the nature of the Neandertal has returned. Brainy or brutish? Man or beast?

Zilhão pointed to the pendant found with Lapedo Child and many other adornments found with Neandertals for his answer. What kind of animal takes the time and energy to make something that is not necessary for survival? What kind of animal can appreciate something solely for its beauty? What kind of animal wears a symbolic statement like a pendant? An intelligent one, Zilhão argued.

And yet not smart enough to hold their own against newcomers.

Who were the Neandertals, really?

Like many archaeological finds, Lapedo Child raises as many questions as he answers. Sometimes, anthropologists will tell you, it's the questions that are the most interesting.

Further reading on Lapedo Child

Shreeve, James. *The Neandertal Enigma: Solving the Mystery of Human Origins.* New York: William Morrow and Company, 1995.

Trinkaus, Erik, and Pat Shipman. *The Neandertals: Changing the Image of Mankind.* New York: Knopf, 1993.

Websites

Australian Museum—Neanderthal Cocktail
http://www.amonline.net.au/archive.cfm?id=405
Contains links to studies of Lapedo Child and other science articles.
S292 Lapedo Child
http://www.open.ac.uk/StudentWeb/s292/S292broadcast_files/lapedo.htm
Find videos and broadcasts of the Lapedo Child discovery here.

Source notes (See Bibliography on p. 178 for full citations.)

"Ooh—this is human!" Kunzig, Robert. "Learning to Love Neanderthals." *Discover* 20, no. 08 (August 1999).

"I immediately recognized something big . . ." Kunzig, Robert. "Learning to Love Neanderthals."

"By Sunday evening we were . . ." Kunzig, Robert. "Learning to Love Neanderthals."

"Email—From: João Zilhão . . ." Zilhão, João, and Erik Trinkaus. *Portrait of the Artist as a Child: The Gravettian Human Skeleton from the Abrigo do Lagar Velho and its Archeological Context.* p. 16.

"I just went away without . . ." Kunzig, Robert. "Learning to Love Neanderthals."

"I wasn't going to leave . . ." Kunzig, Robert. "Learning to Love Neanderthals."

"The end of last week . . ." Zilhão, João. "Fate of the Neandertals." *Archaeology* 53, no. 4 (July/August 2000).
http://www.archaeology.org/0007/abstracts/neandertals.html

"The kid surprised us. . . ."
http://www.sciencenews.org/pages/sn_arc99/ 5_8_99/fob7.htm

"There is an idea that . . ." McKie, Robin. "Did Neanderthals cave in or just get outnumbered?" *London Observer,* September 1, 1998.
http://www.trussel.com/prehist/news70.htm

"They both would have been . . ." Reynolds, Matt. "Neanderthal Love: Scientist Split on Over How Much Mating Occurred." *San Francisco Chronicle,* June 19, 2005.

"only had to produce a . . ." Shreeve, James. *The Neandertal Enigma.*

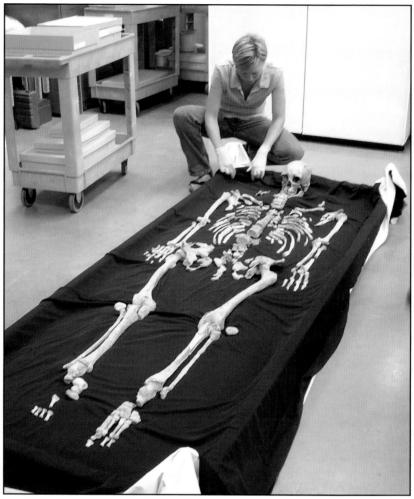

Anthropologist Kari Bruwelheide lays out the assembled and nearly complete skeleton of Kennewick Man. In addition to the bones displayed on this cloth, James Chatters collected more than 200 bone fragments.

Kennewick Man

Discovery

9,000 years ago . . .

The old man limped to the river's edge. He'd lived a good life. He'd been luckier than most, never having suffered the ache of long hunger. A full belly was something to be grateful for—his teeth were worn to stubs from his good fortune.

He'd survived things that would have killed most men. The spear hadn't killed him. Its stone point had lodged in his hip, never letting him forget his luck. The pain followed his every step.

But he'd lived.

The blow that crushed his chest hadn't killed him either. Even though a full, deep breath still felt like a knife through his heart.

But he'd lived.

This time he knew his luck had run out. He was old now, old for his people. They would bury him here next to the slow-moving river—slow-moving like he was these days.

He had one more story left in him. He hoped he'd get a chance to tell it.

July 28, 1996

Eager to watch the boat races at Columbia Park, 21-year-old Will Thomas and his buddies hopped down from the tailgate of their pickup truck. It was getting late, already 2:00 in the afternoon. The races had started long ago. The best spectator spots to watch the hydroplanes were packed 50 people deep. Every year, the Tri-City Sunfest in southeastern Washington State drew more and more people. Tourists flooded in by the thousands. And the Columbia Cup was the highlight of Sunfest.

Entrance fees soared right along with the race's popularity. Fifteen dollars, when they'd already missed so much of the day, seemed too pricey to Thomas. While most of the group coughed up the price of admission, Thomas and two of his friends decided to bypass the ticket booths and sneak in through the bushes.

They hadn't gone far when one of the three decided $15 was a bargain compared to clomping through mushy ground

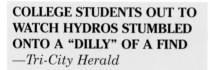

COLLEGE STUDENTS OUT TO WATCH HYDROS STUMBLED ONTO A "DILLY" OF A FIND
—*Tri-City Herald*

in 108-degree heat, thorns snagging his shorts and scratching his legs every step of the way. A machete would have been just the thing to cut through the tangle of olive branches and razor-sharp marsh grasses. He headed back to the ticket booths while Thomas and his buddy Dave Deacy slogged on, determined to get in for free.

After a few minutes in close to 100 percent humidity, with not so much as a breath of cooling breeze, Thomas and Deacy decided their best bet would be to get into the river and wade downstream toward the races. They half slid, half tumbled down the eight-foot clay embankment to the Columbia River. Once in the knee-deep water it was easier going. Their spirits picked up with the roar of the boats. With a cheer Deacy snatched a stick from the water and flung it. *Kerplunk,* it splashed upriver.

They weren't home free yet, though. The river bottom

was mucky. Their feet sunk into the goo, and they had to duck under branches that reached out from the riverbank. Thomas waded farther out. This stretch of the Columbia was wide, shallow, and slow-moving. A few yards offshore the water was still murky, but at least Thomas could see the bottom through the smoky cloud of floating silt. He picked his way along, watching for rusted cans and shards of glass that might cut his bare feet.

Thomas was choosing where to step when he spotted a smooth, round rock the size of a human head. He decided it would be fun to pull a prank on Deacy.

"Hey," he called to Deacy, pointing into the choppy water, "we have a human head."

Deacy waded to where Thomas stood jabbering about having found a murder victim.

Thomas was waiting for Deacy to get close. He planned to pluck the rock out of the water and spook his friend.

Laughing, Thomas scooped up the slimy rock. The mud let go with a slurp. The rock oozed mud from its eye sockets.

The rock had teeth.

❖ ❖ ❖

Thomas and Deacy knew they should turn the skull over to the police. What if it really was the skull of a murder victim? But they also knew that if they turned the skull in now, there would be endless questions. They would miss the races. Thomas waded toward shore to find a place to hide the skull until the races were over.

Late that afternoon Thomas and Deacy met up with their friends in the parking lot. It must have been quite a surprise when the boys came out of the thicket carrying a skull.

It was time to turn the skull over to the police. The boys rummaged through the pickup, looking for something to carry it in. Thomas found a five-gallon paint bucket, dumped out the tools, put the skull in the plastic container, and set off to find a police officer. There were a number of officers managing the crowds at the races. Imagine their surprise when a group of college students walked up with a skull in a bucket. Within seconds walkie-talkies were crackling.

Police Sergeant Craig Littrell took control of the investigation. It was 7:00 p.m. by then, with only an hour of daylight left. Littrell radioed the dive-and-rescue team that had been on hand for the races. The patrol boat sped to where the police waited with Thomas and Deacy.

Kennewick Man was discovered near this riverbank on the Columbia River. Currents exposed his bones and scattered them along the shoreline. Most of his skeleton was found in the mud between the riverbank and the grass in the foreground of this photograph.

The boys led the crew to the spot where they'd found the skull. The boat trolled the area. The police, peering into the water, spotted bones—human bones. Deacy pointed out the stick he'd thrown earlier. It was no stick. It was a thighbone.

Kennewick Man's bones were camouflaged by the river bottom's silt. Unless you knew what you were looking for, this piece of his lower right femur could easily be mistaken for a mud-coated tree root.

Littrell called the coroner and then ordered the area taped off. This could be a crime scene. He didn't want it disturbed any more than it already had been.

One look at the skull, and the coroner knew he'd need an expert. He'd seen enough bones to know that this skull was unusual. He wanted someone who knew bones. The first person who came to mind was anthropologist James Chatters.

Chatters had started his field experience earlier than most. He was a toddler when his father, a botany professor, took him fossil collecting. At age 11 Chatters spent his summer vacation excavating a bison kill site. He'd worked as an archaeologist in the Pacific Northwest for 40 years. When Chatters opened his own archaeological business, he did a little bit of everything. His shingle, if he had hung one, would have read "archaeologist, paleoecologist, forensic anthropologist, and jack-of-all paleo-trades." The man knew bones.

At Columbia Park, Sergeant Littrell led Chatters and the county coroner to the patrol boat. In the northwest, Rattlesnake Mountain loomed deep purple against the red-streaked sky. In the fading light, the olive trees stood like mourners cloaked in black, bent over the river, weeping. It was the perfect stage for bone collecting.

Chatters was surprised when the engine slowed to an idle only a few hundred yards upstream. He carefully studied the area, fixing in his mind what scholars call "the context of discovery." Chatters noted the thick vegetation along the bank—orchard grass, milkweed, thistle, cattails, and olive trees. He noted the debris in the knee-deep water—horseshoes, nails, cracked glass medicine bottles, tin cans, broken willowware ceramic plates, and the skulls of sheep and deer.

Later Chatters wrote in his field diary, "Bone visible in failing light some 15 feet from cut bank in fine beach sand."

They worked quickly, collecting bone fragments—vertebrae and bits of legs, arms, and ribs. By the way the bones were scattered, Chatters guessed that the skeleton had washed out of the bank.

When it got dark, the rescue team turned on a high-beam searchlight they used for night rescues. Chatters, searching within the confines of the narrow beam, handed his finds to the coroner—chunks of a cheekbone, part of a lower jaw. As the beam cut through the murk to the bottom, it bounced off a pelvis bone.

Once they had loaded the bones into the coroner's Jeep and started back to Chatters's place, the coroner asked, "What do you think now?"

Chatters was reluctant to specu-late. "It's going to take some time to figure out."

The coroner was curious; Chatters must have an educated guess. "What do you think so far, though, with what you have?"

"If I had to make a call right now . . . with the association with all that historical trash, I'd say this was a member of a pioneer family."

After unloading the Jeep and saying good night to the coroner, Chatters spread the bones out on a folding table downstairs in his split-level home. He covered them with plastic so they would dry slowly. Turning off the light, he stood for a moment, wondering, *What's your story, old man?*

Monday, July 29, 1996

When Chatters read the morning paper, he couldn't help but laugh—state crime lab indeed; pretty fancy name for his basement office. Downstairs he pulled back the plastic sheet to get a better look at the bones.

When he examined the pelvis, Chatters noticed an odd gray shape beneath the crust of sand coating the ilium—the broad area of spongy bone where the major muscles in the leg and back attach to the pelvis. Chatters tapped the gray spot with a dental pick—*tap, tap, tap. Not bone,* he thought, *harder. A rock?* It was difficult for Chatters to see the object.

It had penetrated the bone, and then the bone had healed over whatever this gray thing was.

It was unthinkable to cut into the bone to remove the object. If the bones ended up belonging to a Native American, then the tribes would want them returned intact. Some Native Americans believe that the Creator will one day summon the dead. To them it is essential that the skeleton remain whole so that the person can live again.

Chatters wondered what the gray object could be. Was it a piece of shrapnel in the hip of a Civil War soldier? Was it a piece of stone from a blasting accident in the hip of a miner? Or could it be a spear point in the hip of one of the first Americans? Chatters needed a closer look. He called Kennewick General Hospital and made an appointment to x-ray the pelvis.

Chatters worked up a profile of the Kennewick skeleton. The sturdiness of the bones and the shape of the pelvis indicated they belonged to a male. Measuring the arm bone, Chatters calculated that the man was about five feet nine inches tall and middle-aged, 50 at most, at the time of death. The skull's shape looked distinctly European. He wished he had more bone to be sure. With several hours to spare before the x-ray appointment, Chatters decided to return to the Columbia River for another look.

When Chatters arrived at Columbia Park, he was thrilled to find that the water level had dropped a good two feet. The shallow edge of the river was now a wide muddy beach exposing bones that the dark water had hidden the night before. The scattered bones reminded him of driftwood. He picked his way around rubber tires and old shoes to collect the bones that were lying on top of the mud. And then, probing the silt with his fingers, he searched for more.

Chatters collected dozens of fragments, feeling lucky to

find some of the small bones from the hands and feet. But the prize was the hinge of the lower jaw, the part that attaches the jaw to the cranium. Turning it over in his hand, Chatters noticed it was narrow and angled back sharply from the part of the jaw that holds the teeth. This led Chatters to believe the jaw belonged to a European or perhaps an African. Native American jaws are broader and have an angle closer to 90 degrees.

That evening at the hospital, Chatters stood behind the radiation barrier, watching the x-ray technician change the film. The tech slid the film cassette into a slot, repositioned the pelvis on the table, and then joined Chatters behind the shield to take the x-ray. When the film was developed, Chatters was disappointed. The picture showed nothing more than a milky haze. The tech adjusted the machine, lowering the radiation intensity. The tech explained to Chatters that the radiation

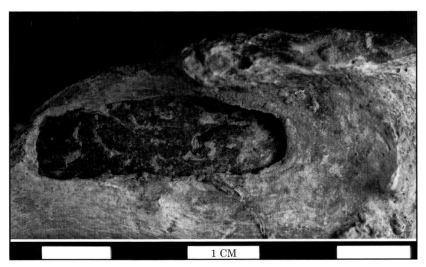

1 CM

The stone spearhead is embedded in Kennewick Man's hipbone. The bone had continued to grow, curving around the stone.

levels in a hospital were calibrated for real people—live bones—not this dried-up chunk of pelvis sitting on the table.

"Nothing will show if it's stone," the tech said.

Stone is made up largely of silica. Silica is what's used to make glass. X-rays "see" through it just like glass. Bone, on the other hand, is made up of calcium and potassium, which are metals. While Chatters could see the details of the pelvic bone, there was nothing more than a ghost where the gray object should have appeared. Whatever it was, it was made out of stone.

Before he left the hospital, Chatters scheduled another appointment for the pelvis—this time for a CT scan. While x-rays take flat, head-on pictures, CT scans revolve around the subject, imaging slice after slice after slice. A computer puts all the slices together to create a three-dimensional picture. The stone might still show up as a ghost, but it would be a three-dimensional ghost.

That night Chatters wrote in his diary, "No luck. Just gray object, can't see form."

Tuesday, July 30, 1996

Chatters went downstairs to the "crime lab" early. Selecting a wooden probe with a fine point and some hydrochloric acid from his equipment shelf, he set to work. First he diluted the acid so that it wouldn't damage the bone. Then he dribbled the acid onto the sand that had cemented itself to the pelvis and the gray object. When the effervescence died down, Chatters carefully scraped away the softened sand. He patiently repeated the process again and again.

With the sand gone, Chatters could make out beveled ridges on the stone. These marks, called flake scars, come from smacking one stone with another to make a tool. This was not shrapnel, nor was it a random chip from a mine explosion. It was a spear point. And from the looks of it, it was ancient. Chatters needed to consult with a stone tool specialist, because if this point was as old as he thought it might be, then this Kennewick Man was no pioneer.

It was time to dot all the i's and cross all the t's. Chatters applied for a permit. The paperwork should have been filled out the moment they knew the death was not recent. It's a crime to collect fossils or artifacts or any archaeological material from federal land without a permit. He faxed a letter to the Army Corps of Engineers, the branch of government that owned the land along Columbia Park, asking for permission to conduct a forensic investigation. He predated the request to cover the bones already recovered.

> In order to solve issues of age and racial affiliation, it may be necessary to revisit the site of the find and obtain more skeletal material from eroded sediments and to inspect the cut bank from which the bones apparently weathered. Since the land is owned by the U.S. Army Corps of Engineers, I am requesting an ARPA permit for the period between July 28, when the remains were turned over to me, and August 3, a period of one week.
> —Application for ARPA permit

Scholars don't whip out a steel tape and measure bones the same way you would measure lumber. The instruments they use are specialized and expensive. Chatters didn't own the necessary tools, but he knew someone who did. To measure Kennewick Man's bones, Chatters called on a colleague he'd known since his college days. Physical anthropologist Catherine MacMillan was as tough as she was thorough.

When Chatters walked into her consulting business, the Bone-Apart Agency, he unloaded the boxes of bones and spread skull fragments and leg bones over the work surface. Not wanting the spear point to scream "paleo-Indian" and influence MacMillan's opinion, Chatters kept the pelvis in the box.

"See what you think," he said. "I need an opinion on race." And with that, Chatters walked out, leaving her to the business of measuring.

❖ ❖ ❖

"Male Caucasian," MacMillan said when Chatters returned.

"You sure?"

"Easy call." There was no doubt in MacMillan's voice.

Chatters asked about the face.

"White guy," she answered.

Chatters asked about the jaw.

"White guy," she repeated.

Chatters asked about the leg bone.

"White guy!" MacMillan said, losing patience.

Before he made MacMillan too mad, Chatters pulled the pelvis out of the box. "Does this change your thinking?"

❖ ❖ ❖

The CT scanner clicked and hummed as the pelvis disappeared into the machine. The computer assembled the x-rays into a three-dimensional image. The spear point was larger than Chatters had expected. It was two inches long, almost an inch wide, and shaped like a willow leaf. The tip was missing. The stone was deeply imbedded in Kennewick Man's hip.

That night Chatters sketched the point in his diary and

wrote, "Appears to be a lance point with point end broken before entry. Really sliced its way in!"

The skeleton was an enigma. The bones had Caucasian characteristics completely different from the features of the Native Americans who lived in the Pacific Northwest at the time spear points like the one in the pelvis were made. Yet the spear point was there. Could someone who looked like Kennewick Man have been in the Americas so long ago? The only way to find out was to carbon-date the skeleton, a test that pinpoints age of organic material by counting carbon atoms. All that's needed to run this test is a bit of organic matter—something that was once living. It can be a bit of wood, leather, or even charcoal. Or it can be a bit of bone.

Plants absorb carbon-14 during photosynthesis. Animals and humans absorb carbon-14 when they eat plants. Carbon-14 happens to be a radioactive isotope, and radioactive isotopes decay in an overall regular manner.

Radioactive isotopes have what's called a half-life. A half-life is the time it takes for half of the isotope to decay. Carbon-14's half-life is about 5,700 years. Start with a cup of carbon-14, and in 5,700 years you'll only have half a cup. In another 5,700 years you'll be down to a quarter cup. After about 50,000 years of half disappearing again and again, there won't be enough carbon-14 left to measure. So for things older than 50,000 years, other methods of dating are used.

All living things contain carbon-12 as well as carbon-14, and they contain these isotopes at a constant ratio. The ratio may be one carbon-14 atom for every trillion carbon-12 atoms, but it is constant. When a living thing stops living, it stops absorbing carbon. The radioactive carbon (the carbon-14) starts to decay. But because carbon-12 is not radioactive, it stays the same. By comparing the number of atoms of carbon-12 to the number of atoms of carbon-14 that remain, scientists can determine a precise time of death.

The problem was that some of Kennewick Man's bone would have to be destroyed to run the test. And to do that meant outraging the tribes.

❖ ❖ ❖

Now that Chatters had his permit, he returned to Columbia Park to recover as much of the skeleton as possible. He set up a screen in a clump of dried grass on the riverbank and slogged through the muck and knee-deep water with buckets full of sediment. It was exhausting work. One bucket of mud from the river bottom required ten buckets of water to wash the slimy goop through the sieve. Chatters's arms and back ached, he was making a mess of the screening area, and he wasn't finding much of anything. He'd raised so much of the fine silt that it clouded the water. He could no longer see the bottom. He worried he would step on and break the fragile facial bones that he was hoping to find. It was time to re-think the operation.

The wave action created by the race boats had exposed the bones before. It might just work again. Chatters waded out and filled his bucket with water. He sloshed water toward the shoreline ten times and then waited for the water to drain away. The very first "wave" exposed two vertebrae and a chunk of jawbone. Each successive wave uncovered more. The lighter bones flipped and rolled onto the beach.

Sunburned, waterlogged, and exhausted, Chatters col-lected most of the skeleton that afternoon. Now he had to decide which of those bones he would send out to be dated. Which part of the body would he have to destroy?

First he researched testing sites to find the laboratory that could do the dating with the least amount of bone. Removing any bone at all would upset many tribal members, but for the sake of his own conscience, Chatters hoped to minimize the damage.

He discovered a lab that could perform the test with a piece of bone the size of a shelled sunflower seed. He still had to decide *which* bone. Chatters reasoned that a toe or finger bone would be the least offensive loss to a person in the next life, and so he chose a bit of bone that connected the little finger to the wrist. He had found the bone when he was cleaning the inside of the skull. A mouse had probably pulled it inside. Skulls make solid, cozy mouse homes and are often chosen by rodents for just that purpose.

Scott Turner, James Chatters' intern, searches the shoreline for Kennewick Man's remains.

The bone Chatters picked turned out to be in excellent condition. The scientists at the lab assured him that the collagen in the bone would give an accurate date. In fact it had been so well preserved that they believed Chatters should consider running DNA tests on it to determine Kennewick Man's race. There was the expense, of course. Chatters had already forfeited his consulting fee to cover the expense of the carbon-dating test. A DNA test was even more expensive. It was something to think about.

August 24, 1996

Chatters was standing at the top of the stairs of the "state crime lab" in his split-level home when the phone rang.

"Hi, Jim. We have your date."

"How'd it come out?"

"Are you sitting down?"

> **TRI-CITY SKELETON DATED AT 9,000 YEARS OLD**
> —*Tri-City Herald*

Deductions
Kennewick Man

Kennewick Man's final tale unfolds

Bioanthropologists study skeletons. They measure millions of bones, looking for similarities and differences in populations. How do male skeletons differ from female skeletons? How do people in one area of the globe differ from those in another area? How do bones change as they age? What do bones look like when an individual gets sick? Or hurt? These are just a few of the questions bones can answer.

Kennewick Man's bones were telling scientists a story, but like any good story it had a few unexpected twists. The biggest surprise was the shape of Kennewick Man's skull. Scholars expected to see Native American features. But when they held Kennewick Man's cranium in one of the standard positions for

> **BONES TELL ANCIENT TALE OF KENNEWICK MAN**
> —*Associated Press*

comparing skulls, the eye sockets lined up all wrong. The nose stuck out too much. The traits weren't Native American at all.

The scientists looked for characteristics found in modern American Indians. Present-day American Indians typically have short, round skulls with broad, flat faces. Kennewick Man's skull was long and narrow with a narrow face and cheekbones that angled back. Nor was the back of his head flattened from being carried on a cradle board from infancy.

This was not at all what scholars expected in an ancient skeleton found in the Pacific Northwest.

Scientists measured the bones to see if the skeleton belonged to a male or a female. To determine gender, the first set of bones scientists look at is the pelvis. Female pelvises are low and broad—shaped for supporting a growing fetus and giving birth. Males have high, narrow pelvises.

Male and female skulls are shaped differently, too. Male skulls are larger and more elongated, with a forehead that slopes back at a sharper angle. Their browridge sticks out farther, and the upper rims of their eye sockets are thicker. Male chins tend to be wide and square. In general, male bones are robust, and because males have greater muscle mass, their bones bulge more where the muscles attach. Kennewick Man was all guy.

Age can be tough to tell. Most age markers, such as tooth eruptions, that were so instrumental in determining Turkana Boy's age, are over and done with by our early 20s. Kennewick Man was long out of his 20s. For someone as old as Kennewick Man, scientists examine the skull for clues.

The human skull is made up of 21 bones, or plates, that grow separately until adulthood. The human brain grows as we age, and the face changes shape. The plates can move independently to accommodate those changes. Around middle to late 20s, narrow bridges begin to knit the plates together. As we get older, the bridges broaden and interconnect until, sometime in middle age, the plates are completely fused. By the time we reach old age, the plates are so tightly woven together that the skull looks like solid bone. This stage is called obliteration. Kennewick Man was obliterated. But the skull is not a precise age indicator. The best the scientists could do was give a rather wide age range: Kennewick Man

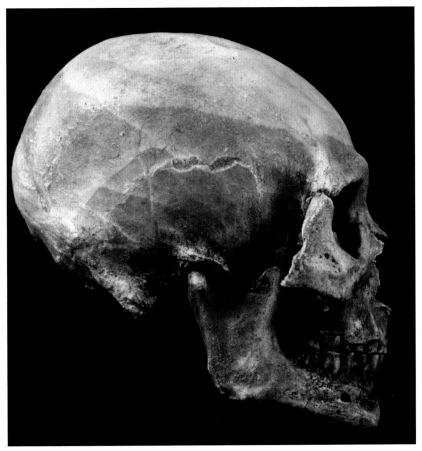

Kennewick Man's skull surprised scientists with its prominent chin, projecting nose, protruding upper jaw, and face positioned far forward in front of the braincase. These are features more common in modern European skulls than in modern Native American skulls.

died when he was somewhere between 35 and 50 years of age.

Scientists measured the long bones, the arm and leg bones, to calculate Kennewick Man's height. They simply had to plug those numbers into a formula. But which formula? There are different equations for different populations.

The set of height formulas that many scientists use was put together by an anatomist during wartime. The U.S. Armed Forces runs a human identification lab for war casualties. During the Korean War the lab's anatomist compared the lengths of the long bones of the victims to the victims' heights listed in their military records. From those measurements he came up with formulas specific to several different ethnic groups. But Kennewick Man came from a time before those groups existed. Which population would be a good model?

To pick the best formula for Kennewick Man, scholars decided to calculate the ratio of femur to tibia and compare that to the ratio of femur to tibia in different populations. They measured his femur, the long bone from the hip to the knee, and his tibia, the larger of the two bones from the knee to the ankle, to get Kennewick Man's ratio. Which population's ratio matched Kennewick Man's? The closest value was for Central American Indians. Applying this formula, Kennewick Man stood five feet nine inches tall, confirming Chatters's earlier estimate made from the arm bone.

Teeth record our medical history. Kennewick Man had no cavities and only a bit of tartar buildup. His teeth were worn, but not unusually so for someone his age. Kennewick Man's teeth showed that he had had a healthy childhood.

Bones are good indicators of a person's overall health. Food shortages and poor health impede normal bone growth and show up as white rings on an x-ray. Kennewick Man's healthy teeth and bones showed a childhood without serious problems, but when he turned 15 everything changed. His bones recorded one catastrophe after another.

When scientists discovered Kennewick Man's bone was chipped at the elbow, they speculated that his first accident may have happened because he tried to catch himself when

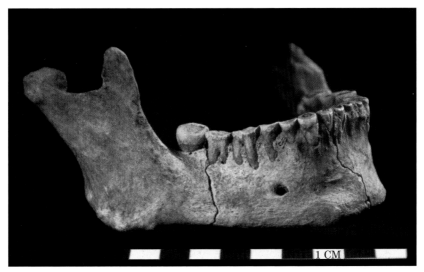
Kennewick Man's teeth were well worn, but in good shape for a man his age.

he fell. After that, pain prevented Kennewick Man from using his left arm. Scientists reasoned that this accident happened around the time he turned 15. If it had happened earlier, then his left arm bones would have been shorter than his right. They were the same length. If the injury had happened much later than 15, then his left arm muscles would have developed fully. Protrusions where the muscles attached to the bone showed that they had not.

Whether it was to compensate for the weak left arm or from a lifetime of hunting and spearfishing, Kennewick Man's right arm was a powerhouse. The muscles were so well developed that they bent his bones.

An orthopedic surgeon who examined Kennewick Man's rib cage noticed seven fractures. "What an impact! We usually see that now when someone has been in a head-on collision and their chest has been driven into the steering wheel."

Had Kennewick Man fallen off a cliff? Had he been kicked by a bison or an elk? Whatever happened, he would have had trouble breathing. His body healed, but from that day forward, breathing deeply or lifting heavy things would always have been painful.

His chest wouldn't have been the only thing that hurt. Years before he died, Kennewick Man had been shot in the hip with a spear. The spear came at him so fast and forcefully that it penetrated his skin and stuck in his pelvis. The germs from the stone point caused an infection in his bone. The stone point sliced blood vessels that nourished the pelvis, so the bone around the stone died. Over time new bone grew around the spear point, but the pain never went away.

Kennewick Man also had a small depression in the left side of his forehead from a scalp wound. From the looks of the bone, the wound had been infected. The infection clogged some of the vessels that fed the bone underneath, causing the bone to die. At some point Kennewick Man must have gotten a good conk on the head. It looks as if he was either clubbed by a right-handed attacker or nailed by a falling rock. By the time Kennewick Man died, his forehead had long healed. At least one of his injuries wouldn't have bothered him.

The poor man's problems didn't end there. Bone tumors blocked both ears, making him hard of hearing. This kind of tumor is often caused by extreme cold. Scientists wonder if during the winter Kennewick Man swam in the frigid Columbia River to fish for food or to relieve his aches and pains and occasional fevers.

Kennewick Man also suffered from arthritis. In his neck the arthritis was so advanced that his bones were polished from rubbing against one another. When he turned his head he probably heard a squeak.

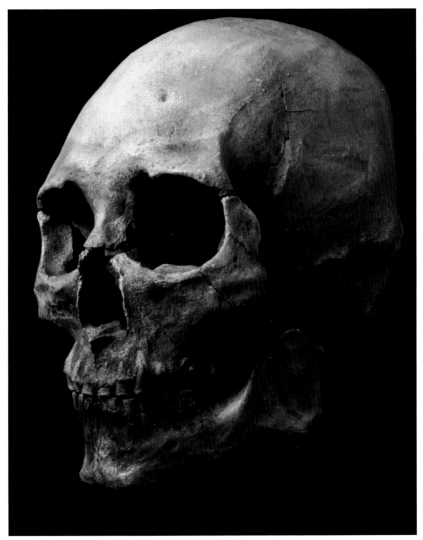

The dot on Kennewick Man's forehead is where he took a blow to the head. The fracture had healed long before Kennewick Man's death.

His right shoulder bone was chipped. He died before it healed. When a bone heals, the new bone is a slightly different texture. Initially scientists thought Kennewick Man's bone at the break was the same texture as the bone else-where, which made them wonder, Did Kennewick Man fall when he died? Or did someone move him soon after death,

while his body was still stiff with rigor mortis? Perhaps a loved one forced his arm to his side while preparing him for burial, causing the shoulder bone to chip. But more recent studies reveal some minor healing had occurred which casts suspicion on Kennewick Man's cause of death.

Smithsonian's forensic anthropologist Doug Owsley said, "This guy is really trying to tell us his story."

What did Kennewick Man look like?

One of the most sensitive questions asked of the bones was, What did Kennewick Man look like? During the short time James Chatters had the skeleton stretched across his lab table, he had tried to find out. Chatters made a mold of the skull. From that mold he cast a plastic head.

Armed with modeling clay, sculptor's wax, and sculpting tools, Chatters built Kennewick Man's face from the inside out. He studied anatomy books. He studied photographs of skinned cadaver faces. Pictures of skulls with the location of muscle attachments clearly labeled were most helpful.

A few places where the facial muscles had attached to Kennewick Man's skull protruded more than normal. Chatters noticed that these were the muscles that push the lower lip up and out and raise the upper lip from the cheekbone. Contract-ing those muscles on his own face, Chatters discovered the look on Kennewick Man's face. It was the look of a man in pain. A colleague told Chatters, "This guy cried a lot."

Chatters molded sculptor's wax into muscles and pressed

James Chatters (left) and Tom McClelland (right) reconstruct Kennewick Man's face in clay. The square jaw and prominent chin are not features consistent with American Indian peoples.

them onto the plastic skull. He placed 17 muscles on each side of the face. There were O-shaped sphincter muscles encircling the mouth and eyes. There were delicate muscles that allow people to wrinkle their nose, wiggle their eyebrows, and smile or frown. And there were the massive muscles that can turn a jaw into a nutcracker. Chatters layered them on.

When he was satisfied with the positions of all the muscles, Chatters rolled out sheets of modeling clay like pie crust and draped them over the face. Kennewick Man would have the sags and wrinkles that come with age, and so Chatters added those. He carved the scar in Kennewick Man's forehead and built a big nose that matched the nasal opening in the cast. He didn't add hair because he had no way of knowing its color or texture. And for the same reasons, Chatters didn't color the clay. There was no way to know the color of Kennewick Man's skin.

How was Kennewick Man buried?

Some scientists believe that like Lapedo Child, Kennewick Man had been purposely buried. They concluded that his people placed him in a grave two to three feet deep, face up, with his head higher than his feet, and his hands at his sides. Residue on the underside of his bones showed scientists exactly how he was positioned in the dirt. But science is all about different points of view. Chatters, and others, don't believe burial is consistent with the geological evidence. They don't see a corpse neatly laid to rest. They see legs askew and earth above him far too recent to have been placed by gravediggers.

THE LAST DAYS OF KENNEWICK MAN
—Washington Associated Press

Scientists do agree that the only scrapes on Kennewick Man's bones were fresh. From this, scientists could tell that his skeleton had been undisturbed until recently. The water rushing past pulled away the fine silt that had so perfectly preserved him and left its mark. Kennewick Man had lain for thousands of years with his left side closest to the river and his head pointing upstream.

What would happen to him now that he was no longer protected by the earth?

> Kennewick Man lived along the Columbia River 450 generations ago in a culture now forgotten, speaking a language now dead, among a people who may be extinct. . . . what should become of Kennewick Man's remains?
> —James Chatters, *Ancient Encounters*

Debates
Kennewick Man

Why battle over bones?

Burying the dead—it's a ritual anthropologists like to trot out to pinpoint when our ancestors crossed over to humanity. It took an act of Congress in 1990, the Native American Graves Protection and Repatriation Act (NAGPRA), to protect Native American peoples' right to that basic act of humanity. For centuries sacred cemeteries had been strip-mined for human remains and grave goods in the name of science. Some of the most offensive looting was carried out on 19th-century battlefields by soldiers who were following orders from the Army's surgeon general to collect skulls and send them to the Smithsonian. Museum and university vaults overflowed with the bones of some 100,000 to 200,000 individuals. Grave robbers and private collectors pillaged countless more. NAGPRA's purpose was to correct this national disgrace.

> These are the remains of someone that we cherish as one
> of our own. . . . We bow our head in shame and sorrow for
> the treatment of the remains of the Ancient One.
> —Confederated Tribes of the Colville Reservation

NAGPRA provided a process for the return of the remains of Native American ancestors to their tribal descendants, and it outlined how future excavations were to be handled. Skeletons from as long ago as the Ancient One—the name American Indians gave Kennewick Man—would test NAGPRA. The battle over the bones boiled down to two basic questions: Is a skeleton that's more than 9,000 years old Native American? Is it possible to prove a connection between Kennewick Man and a modern tribe?

> As a specialist in the prehistory of the western North America, I can assure you that no living society, Native American or other, can credibly claim biological or cultural affiliation with archaeological remains 93 centuries old. This life span represents 500 generations. During this time, peoples entered the New World, moved extensively within it, evolved culturally, intermarried, and sometimes died out. The true descendants of people represented by Kennewick Man might be living in Central or South America, or might be extinct.
> —California archaeologist

> We don't accept any artificial cut-off date set by scientists to separate us from our ancestors. What Europeans want to do with their dead is their business; we have different values.
> —Pawnee attorney

Where does Kennewick Man belong?

The law according to NAGPRA was clear—removal of Native American remains from federal land without a permit was a crime. Kennewick Man was found on federal land. The coroner who had taken the bones to Chatters in the first place was ordered to seize Kennewick Man under the terms of the Archaeological Resources Protection Act and turn his bones over to the Army Corps of Engineers.

Chatters padded a plywood crate with bubble wrap, laying the heaviest bones in first. He placed the braincase next to the leg and arm bones. He packaged the smaller bones and fragments in plastic bags so they wouldn't get misplaced. While he worked, he worried about what science was losing. So much could have been learned from this one man, but instead the bones were headed for destruction. Once buried, they would rapidly decompose until nothing was left. With one last longing look, Chatters placed the lid on the box and screwed it in place, thinking, *I have failed him. I have failed posterity.*

Although belief systems vary from tribe to tribe, all Native Americans have respect for the remains of the dead. The Spirit Journey is part of traditional Native beliefs. The journey is the passage from life on Mother Earth to the next place. The journey continues until the bones have decomposed. If the skeleton is disturbed, the journey is interrupted. Until the bones are *completely* returned to the earth, the ancestor has no place in this life or the next. If no ancestors complete the journey, there will be no one to come to Native ceremonies and guide the living. When ancestral remains end up being used for highway fill, as they did in Illinois, it's no wonder American Indians fear for their future.

While the Army Corps of Engineers tried to discover which tribe Kennewick Man should be turned over to, Chatters campaigned to stop the reburial. He called his colleagues. They encouraged him to notify archaeologists who were opposed to reburial and to lobby senators and members of Congress. The Corps was besieged and barraged. It refused comment and doggedly moved forward with plans to rebury Kennewick Man.

Many (but not all) archaeologists fought against reburial because they were alarmed by the number of priceless bones reburied and destroyed by the earth—knowledge lost.

Many (but not all) Native Americans fought for reburial because they were alarmed by the number of sacred bones unearthed and violated—loved ones lost.

Bonnichsen et al v. U.S.

Two days before Kennewick Man's scheduled reburial, eight scientists joined forces and sued the Army Corps of Engineers. Even though the judge denied the scientists' motion for a temporary restraining order to prevent Kennewick Man's reburial, the Corps was unable to move forward with its plans. Claims for Kennewick Man were coming in from several tribes, and according to the law, the Corps was required to investigate them all.

The judge ordered the Corps to give the scientists a 10-day notice if its investigation ended with a decision to bury Kennewick Man. Ten days would give the scientists the opportunity to reopen their lawsuit.

The judge asked the scientists' lawyer, "What if you thought this was a skeleton of one of your ancestors?"

"If it were one of mine?" she replied.

"Yes."

It was the open door the lawyer had been waiting for. "Anthropologists who had a look at it . . . believe that the evidence says this was a wanderer who is not a lineal ancestor of any modern-day person in this country. He doesn't belong to any of us," she responded.

With those words the legal battle over the bones began, and for months, then years, it dragged on.

The Smithsonian submitted an official request for Kennewick Man, citing an 1846 law that required materials of historical significance found on federal land to be turned over to the museum. Government attorneys countered by citing laws that made it illegal for one branch of the federal government (the Smithsonian) to sue another branch of the federal government (the Corps).

The scientists requested access to the skeleton and

Matt Wuerker's cartoon offers humorous commentary on the battle fought over Kennewick Man's skeleton, including stereotyped portrayals of the different political groups with an interest in this discovery.

presented the court with a plan for study—bones to be measured, examined, and tested.

The judge denied access, but he ordered the Corps to answer 17 questions that would help him decide if and how NAGPRA applied to Kennewick Man. One question—"Are scientific study and reburial mutually exclusive?"—was clearly fishing for some middle ground. But as the trial continued, the sides became more polarized. There would be no middle ground.

News reached the scientists that the Corps hadn't been taking proper care of Kennewick Man. He was still in the plywood crate Chatters had packed over a year before. The Corps had allowed Native ceremonies to be performed over the bones. They were coated in ashes and cedar boughs and had been mixed with animal bones. Not only were they contaminated with bacteria, but nothing had been done to preserve them. The Corps hadn't even bothered to document who had visited, a fact made more alarming by the discovery that some of the bones were missing.

The judge granted a hearing over Kennewick Man's negligent care and lack of security. It did little for the judge's disposition that after all these months the Corps showed up unable to answer a single one of his 17 questions. He ordered the Corps to take an immediate inventory of the bones with two scientists present. All objections were overruled.

❖ ❖ ❖

It had been two years since Chatters had last seen Kennewick Man. He wasn't sure which of them was the worse for wear. The cracks in Kennewick Man's cranium had grown longer and wider. Leg bones were missing, and the bones that remained were dry and cracking. The judge had ordered Kennewick Man transferred to a neutral site. Chatters hoped this would happen quickly—for Kennewick Man's sake.

❖ ❖ ❖

In an effort to answer the judge's questions, the Corps conducted its own studies in secret for months. Nothing so far linked Kennewick Man to any modern tribe. Failure to make the necessary tribal connection required by NAGPRA meant losing the court battle. It was clear that the only way to comply with the judge's order to answer those 17 questions was to carbon-date and run a DNA test on Kennewick Man.

From the start, the testing was a fiasco. Ignoring advice to take tiny samples from different bones to find those that were best preserved, the Corps's experts took a rotary saw to Kennewick Man. They hacked a chunk out of Kennewick Man's shin and sawed his foot in two. One distressed witness reported, "There was bone dust flying everywhere, and the cutting just seemed to go on and on for about twenty minutes. They had to keep stopping to wipe their goggles so they could see to work."

No one was happy. The Native Americans felt helpless to protect their dead from desecration, even though the law was supposed to be on their side. The scientists felt helpless to protect a potential source of knowledge from being obliterated by carelessness and incompetence.

The worst of it was that after they had butchered his bones, the samples taken were too poorly preserved to give definitive results. DNA test results were inconclusive. But the radiocarbon dates did back up Chatters's earlier test results, confirming Kennewick Man to be somewhere between 8,340 and 9,200 years old.

Too old, the courts decided, to be linked to any modern tribe.

I'm absolutely thrilled that the court has affirmed the public's right to knowledge and rejected this attempt, on religious grounds, to limit scientific inquiry.
  —James Chatters

We are disappointed in this decision and are concerned about the ability of NAGPRA to protect Native American burials and remains, as intended by Congress.
  —Confederated Tribes of the Colville Reservation

When did humans enter the race?

One of the key questions the court faced when coming to a decision had to do with race. What makes a Native American a Native American?

From the beginning the press had misunderstood Chatters when he said Kennewick Man was "Caucasian-like." It was a misunderstanding that would haunt him for years. The mistake was not so different from one the press had made more than a century before with Charles Darwin. For decades people misconstrued Darwin's words, claiming he said that humans descended *from* apes. That was not at all what Darwin wrote. Darwin's theory proposed that humans and apes shared a common ancestor. Chatters had suggested that Kennewick Man and Europeans shared a common ancestor, not that Kennewick Man himself was of European descent. But this did not sit any more comfortably than Darwin's assertion had.

The press latched onto Chatters's description of Kennewick Man's skull as "Caucasian-like" (or "European," when he thought he was looking at a pioneer). They led their readers to points Chatters never intended. Even if Chatters believed in the existence of human races, he would certainly not have believed that those same races existed 10,000 years ago. Nor was he trying to suggest that Europeans were in the Americas before Native American ancestors. When it comes to the notion of race, emotions flare. Misinterpreting Chatters's use of the word *Caucasian* added fuel to the fire.

The idea of race is useful to botanists. Plants behave differently depending on where in the world they grow. Race categorizes those differences. But race doesn't translate well when it's applied to humans.

When humans left Africa some 50,000 years ago and dispersed across the globe, they split from one population into many populations. These smaller populations continued to evolve, each in its own way, reacting to unique environments. Each population was nudged along its own evolutionary path. Climate, disease, warfare, and adaptations to new foods and lands all influenced how the population evolved.

Races supposedly arose from independent populations that were separated geographically. The problem is that human populations aren't all that different. The biological definition of race requires that the races differ genetically from one another by more than 30 percent. Human "races" differ genetically by no more than 15 percent. In fact there is a greater genetic variation *within* human "races" than between them. So biologically speaking, for humans, race doesn't exist. Scientists have discarded outdated thinking that all people belong to one of three races—Caucasoid, Mongoloid, or Negroid—and now use the term "ethnic group" as a more accurate description of human differences.

❖ ❖ ❖

Forensic scientists like James Chatters identify a skull's ethnic group by comparing it to skulls in reference collections. These skull libraries contain thousands of skulls collected from cemeteries, teaching hospitals, and morgues. Comparisons work well for identifying a skull found at a modern crime scene, or even a skull of a European pioneer living a few centuries ago, but when the skull is as old as Kennewick Man's, all bets are off. Human skulls didn't *begin* to develop many of the features we see in modern populations until about 12,000 years ago.

So it would have been a surprise if Kennewick Man *had* looked like a modern Native American. When the first people migrated into the Americas, they separated from their ancestral population. Isolated geographically, they continued to evolve. Over many generations these small, separate populations, buffeted by changes in the American landscape, drifted genetically away from the parent population. Diet changes from climate swings, plant and animal extinctions, and the advent of farming altered skull shape. Devastating diseases brought to the Americas by the Europeans altered skull shape. Modern western habits and diet will alter skull shape. Skulls have been changing since the first people set foot in the Americas.

Who were the first Americans?

There are several theories about who came first, and they all revolve around *how* those first people got here. Until recently the most popular theory was the Clovis-first theory.

The Clovis-first theory has a small band of big-game hunters—at most 150 of them—trekking from Siberia into Alaska about 13,500 years ago. Their travel date is a critical factor in this model. Any earlier and it would have been a death march across lifeless sheets of ice. About 13,500 years ago, though, the glaciers began to melt, exposing an ice-free corridor where grass sedges and sagebrush took precarious hold.

Once the ice age hunters made it across the blustery pass, they must have been amazed by their good fortune. The vast uninhabited land was a hunter-gatherer's dream—unlimited game, lush growth, and no competition for either one. They spread out fast, occupying North America in just a few centuries and arriving at the tip of South America just a few centuries after that. Not bad for a small band of adventurers.

Scholars followed their expansion through the tools they

James Chatters examines Kennewick Man's skull. He will compare his data with measurements compiled in skull libraries.

left behind, first discovered in Clovis, New Mexico. The most distinctive of the tools was the Clovis spear point, an earlier version of the stone point imbedded in Kennewick Man's hip.

Flaws in the Clovis-first theory arose when an archaeologist found evidence of a settlement in southern Chile, complete with human footprints where someone had walked through the mud 14,500 years ago. How did someone get to the tip of South America 1,000 years *before* the glaciers parted? To complicate matters the tool technology at this settlement was not the same as the tool technology found at Clovis. Different tool kits could mean that people were forced to change their methods because of new toolmaking materials. Or it could mean that the people came from somewhere else. If these were not the mammoth hunters from Siberia, then who were they and how did they get there?

One theory that has gained popularity among scientists is the Pacific Rim theory—out with the mammoth hunters, in with the coastal dwellers. Hugging the coastline, these immigrants boated their way south, from Alaska to Central America. Once there, they split up: some headed toward the Atlantic coast, while others continued down to the tip of South America.

Marine ecologists have discovered that there were kelp forests flourishing from Japan to Alaska to southern California at the end of the last ice age. This "kelp highway" would have provided an easy source of food for travelers—the kelp itself and the sea life that feeds off it. Not only would these sea forests have provided all the food travelers needed for a long journey, but the mass of plants would have buffered waves and made travel safer and navigation easier.

Finding proof of shoreline settlements, however, is a challenge. The last ice age had so much of the earth's water trapped in ice that sea levels were 400 feet lower. Coastal plains reached hundreds of miles into what is now ocean. Today any ancient coastal community would be underwater. Archaeologists, who most often dig on a shoestring budget, don't have access to the expensive equipment needed to do deep-sea exploration. One anthropologist lamented to *Time* magazine, "The maritime community is interested in shipwrecks and treasure. A little bit of charcoal and some rock on the ocean floor is not very exciting to them."

There are also theories that haven't gained much popularity among scholars, one being a Columbus-like crossing of the Atlantic Ocean. And we can't overlook the "all of the above" choice. There could have been a variety of migrations—different routes, different times, different peoples. Scientists hope that skeletons like Kennewick Man will provide the evidence that ultimately resolves these debates.

For now Kennewick Man seems to raise more questions than he answers. But only the best stories force us to question, leading us to reexamine ourselves and our thinking. It appears Kennewick Man got to tell his story after all—and like many Native American legends, it is an ongoing tale.

Further reading on Kennewick Man

Chatters, James C. *Ancient Encounters: Kennewick Man and the First Americans*. New York: Simon & Schuster, 2001.

Downey, Roger. *Riddle of the Bones: Politics, Science, Race, and the Story of Kennewick Man*. New York: Copernicus, 2000.

Websites

Kennewick Man/Tri-City Herald: Mid-Columbia News
 http://www.tri-cityherald.com/kman
 Kennewick Man has his own website.

Source notes (See Bibliography on p. 178 for full citations.)

"COLLEGE STUDENTS OUT . . ." Lee, Mike. *Tri-City Herald,* April 4, 2003.

"Hey, we have a human . . ." Stang, John. *Tri-City Herald,* June 20, 2005.

"SKULL LIKELY EARLY WHITE . . ." Schafer, Dave. *Tri-City Herald,* June 20, 2005.

"Bone visible in failing light . . ." Chatters's field diary.

"What do you think now. . . ." *Ancient Encounters,* p. 27.

"SKULL FOUND ON SHORE OF . . ." Stang, John. *Tri-City Herald,* June 20, 2005.

"What's your story, old man?" *Ancient Encounters,* p. 27.

"Nothing will show if it's . . ." *Ancient Encounters,* p. 34.

"No luck. Just gray object. . . ." Chatters's field diary.

"In order to solve issues. . . ." Application for ARPA permit.

"See what you think. . . ." *Ancient Encounters,* p. 37.

"Male Caucasian . . ." *Ancient Encounters,* p. 38.

"Appears to be a lance. . . ." Chatters's field diary.

"Hi, Jim. We have your . . ." *Ancient Encounters,* p. 50.

"TRI-CITY SKELETON DATED AT . . ." Stang, John. *Tri-City Herald,* June 20, 2005.

"BONES TELL ANCIENT TALE. . . ." Associated Press, February 24, 2006. http://www.msnbc.msn.com/id/11532671/

"What an impact!" *Ancient Encounters,* p. 134.

"This guy is really . . ." Doughton, Sandi. *Seattle Times,* July 11, 2005. http://community.seattletimes.nwsource.com/archive/?date=20050711&slug=kennewick11m

"RESEARCHER SEEKS SECRETS OF KENNEWICK. . . ." Rust, Susanne. *Milwaukee Journal Sentinel,* February 1, 2006. http://www.jsonline.com/story/index.aspx?id=389315

"This guy cried a lot." John Gurche to James Chatters. *Ancient Encounters,* p. 145.

"THE LAST DAYS OF KENNEWICK . . ." Washington Associated Press, February 4, 2006. http://www.vnnforum.com/archive/index.php/t-30127.html

"Kennewick Man lived along the . . ." *Ancient Encounters,* p. 269.

"These are the remains of . . ." Kathy Womer, Colville Business Council, Confederated Tribes of the Colville Reservation, 1998.

http://www.washington.edu/burkemuseum/kman/native_american_views.php

"As a specialist in the prehistory . . ." California archaeologist Michael Moratto. http://www.kenanmalik.com/essays/index_knowledge.html

"We don't accept any artificial . . ." Pawnee attorney Walter Echo Hawk Ziff. Rao, Bruce H. and Pratima V. *Borrowed Power Essays on Cultural Appropriation,* p. 299.

"I have failed him. I . . ." *Ancient Encounters,* p. 78.

"What if you thought this . . ." *Riddle of the Bones,* p. 49.

"There was bone dust flying . . ." *Ancient Encounters,* p 114.

"I'm absolutely thrilled. . . ." Paulson, Tom. Seattlepi.com, February 5, 2004. http://www.seattlepi.com/local/159408_kennewickman05.html

"We are disappointed in this. . . ." BBC News, February 5, 2004. Press release, Confederated Tribes of the Colville Reservation. http://news.bbc.co.uk/2/hi/americas/3460773.stm

"The maritime community is interested . . ." Lemonick, Michael D., and Andrea Dorfman. "Who were the First Americans?" *Time* magazine, March 5, 2006. http://www.time.com/time/magazine/article/0,9171,1169905-1,00.html

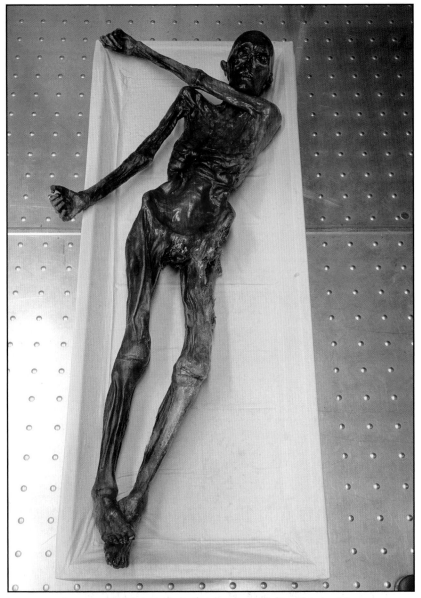

Damage done to Iceman's left hip and thigh by the jackhammer is clearly visible in this picture of his mummified body. He looks as if he is raising his left arm to show off his wound, but it was the glacier that permanently tucked his arm under his chin.

Iceman
Discovery

5,300 years ago . . .

He was an old man now. He'd seen 46 winters come and go, but he wouldn't see another. In the past six months, he'd been sick three times. The last illness had raged for two weeks, but he had recovered.

He had survived frostbite on the little toe of his left foot, broken ribs, and a stroke. He lived with arthritis and hardening of the arteries. His lungs were black from hearth smoke, and his intestines were home to whipworms, which doubled him over with cramping and diarrhea. Fleas tortured him. But none of this would kill him.

In the end he didn't die of old age or sickness. He was murdered. A flint arrowhead shattered his left shoulder blade, rendering his arm useless. A stab wound on his right hand cut clear through his palm between his thumb and forefinger.

High in the Alps, above the tree line, where even the summer sun couldn't rid the mountainside of ice and snow, he stumbled to a spot that would offer him some protection. Near a boulder, in a hollow, he lay down on his stomach. In shock from the loss of blood, he turned his head to the right, never noticing that his left ear had folded over. Three layers of clothing and animal-skin shoes stuffed with grass for insulation were no match for the cold. He froze.

Subfreezing temperatures prevented bacteria, fungi, and insects from ravaging the soft tissue. Dry winds wicked away what little moisture his emaciated body had to offer. A spring snowfall blanketed him, hiding his body from the birds and carnivores that would have picked it to pieces. His skin gradually darkened to orange and over time deepened to nut brown.

Winter came and more snow fell, more than would melt that following summer. Each winter added another layer, compressing everything below it into ice. A glacier formed above him and moved under the force of its own weight. The glacier pushed outward. Tucked into a hollow, the body was protected from the glacier's full weight and moved only slightly as the river of ice above it flowed.

The glacier advanced and retreated, advanced and retreated, rocking the body. The movement deformed the rib cage. It fractured ribs. It broke the left arm and tore a piece of scalp away.

Tension in the ice grew. The glacier groaned with built-up pressure. Crevasses cracked open across the ice, spreading like spider lightning. Summer's melt trickled through breaks in the ice. Seasonal freezes and thaws nudged the old man's belongings. His copper ax, his hide quiver with 14 arrows, two birch-bark containers, the frame of his backpack, all floated away from the body.

A faraway wind blew, carrying a cloud of dust from the Sahara to the old man's high alpine resting place. The dust that coated the glacier in a warm blanket started a melt. A warm spell finished it. The ice around the old man turned to slush. He was trapped from the waist down. But his head, back, and shoulders were exposed. He looked as if he were trying to climb out of the ice.

September 18, 1991

The crevasse yawned in front of Erika and Helmut Simon, its ice walls marbled with gray and brown streaks. The couple inched forward to peer over the edge and into the abyss. The gaping split made them uneasy, even with crampons strapped to their boots and spiked solidly into the ice. All too often in these parts of the Alps, where Italy and Austria touched, mountain climbers and hikers fell into crevasses, only to be chewed up by the glacier and spit out decades later.

The sun was shrinking the glacier. Runoff gurgled and burbled beneath their feet. Hundreds of steady drip, drip, drips drilled tunnels for tiny rivulets that wore even deeper grooves. The Simons picked their way along the length of the crevasse, looking for a place to cross.

A few yards away they found a pinch in the crevasse where the two sides came close enough for them to step across. It wasn't the last detour they would take that day. The glacier had fractured into a maze of cracks, forcing the Simons to change direction again and again. By the time they reached the Similaun summit, they knew there wouldn't be enough daylight for them to make it back to their inn in the valley.

The only shelter they could reach before nightfall was a rustic mountaineer's lodge with no running water. At least they would be warm, and the food and company would be good. After a last look at the choppy sea of jutting mountaintops, Helmut adjusted his white cap and pushed off the rock pile they had been sitting on. A few hours later, just as the first stars pricked the darkening sky, the Simons arrived at the lodge.

The next morning the Simons woke up to a sky so vividly blue it looked more like a painting than the real thing. Erika had her mind set on a hot shower back at the inn, but Helmut felt the pull of a nearby summit, Finail Peak—the second-highest summit in the Ötztal Alps. They could leave their backpacks at the lodge and be at the summit before noon. With a breathtaking day beckoning, Helmut convinced Erika to strike out for Finail Peak.

The Simons joined another couple, and the four scrambled up the craggy mountainside. Here and there a weed had managed to sprout, eking what nourishment it could from the dust and moisture trapped in a crack. This high above the tree line there is no soil for roots to finger, only rock—lots of rock.

By the time the two couples reached Finail Peak, just after noon, the wind had picked up. The couples only stayed a moment on the narrow ledge before parting ways. The Simons headed back to the lodge to pick up their gear.

Erika and Helmut chose a herder's path—one of many that had crisscrossed the mountainside for thousands of years. *A shortcut was just the thing,* they thought. Up ahead Erika spied a pile of rocks with a stick wedged in the top—a trail marker. The trail followed a long trenchlike hollow full of slushy water. They were walking single file, careful to keep their feet dry, when Helmut spotted something nut brown lying on top of the snow. Thinking it was trash, Helmut felt a flash of anger at the thoughtless litterbug. *How could they spoil this untouched land?*

Horrified, Erika backed away. "Look," she stammered, "it's a person."

The body lay facedown in the snow, the lower half disappearing into the ice. The upper half looked as if it were trying to pull itself out of the glacier.

The Simons reported the body to the caretaker at the lodge. The caretaker reported it to the police. Not knowing

It's easy to see how a hiker might mistake this mummy for trash along the trail. With only his head and upper torso free from the ice, Iceman looks more like a crumpled paper bag rather than the remains of a human being.

which side of the border the body was on, he called both the Italian and the Austrian police.

The Italians studied their maps—it looked to them as if the corpse was in Austria. The Austrians came to the same conclusion. This was the sixth body the glacier had given up that season. Grimly the Austrians returned once more to the missing persons reports, wondering which family they would be calling this time.

Meanwhile the caretaker and a kitchen worker set out for the site that the Simons had described. What if the body turned out to be someone who had stayed at their lodge? They steeled themselves for the worst. In little more than an hour, they were standing over the body. The caretaker knew immediately that whoever this was, he'd never been a guest at the lodge.

Leathered skin clung to his backbone and rib cage, outlining every bone, as if he'd been shrink-wrapped in his own skin. He was scrawny and bald and naked. The Simons hadn't mentioned the peculiar items that surrounded the body. On a ledge, four or five steps away, the caretaker found an ax, its blade bound to a weathered wooden handle with leather. Sticks that had no business above the tree line lay scattered and tangled in string. And most revealing, the caretaker found the fur of an animal he knew was extinct. The body had been there awhile.

That evening, based on the caretaker's information, the Austrian police released this statement:

> 19th September 1991—Around 12:00 p.m. climbers coming down from the Finail summit found a partially melted-out corpse . . . based on equipment it is a mountain accident that happened some years ago. . . .

The police suspected that the body might belong to a music professor from Verona who had disappeared while hiking in 1938. The next day Police Inspector Anton Koler intended to investigate.

September 20, 1991

From the ground the caretaker waved to the pilot, signaling a place for him to set the helicopter down near Iceman. Once Inspector Koler had unloaded his gear, the pilot took the chopper to a safer landing spot at a lower altitude.

Iceman startled Koler. Bodies that have been trapped in glaciers usually are deformed by the ice flow. Some bodies shatter, their broken parts jumbled in the movement. Others are stretched flat and rolled out like pie crust. Most often the sheering and grinding forces rip apart the corpses. Iceman wasn't mangled, contorted, or dismembered.

Even more baffling, the skin texture was all wrong. Soft tissues, including skin, that are protected from the air by the glacier usually turn to "grave wax." The skin will look soapy. Or it may look like crumbled feta cheese. It stinks, too.

Iceman's skin wasn't waxy or crumbled at all. It resembled brown leather. Koler didn't smell the familiar ammonia-like odor either. *Never mind,* he thought, *time to get the body out and into the hands of the undertaker before the weather changes.*

Koler assembled a portable jackhammer, which looked like a chisel mounted to the barrel of a pistol. He used it to smash the ice around the corpse. Ice chips sprayed everywhere. It was difficult to see where the tip of the chisel was striking. Bits of grass, leather, and string mixed with the slush.

Koler lay down in the slush next to the body in order to see better. The jackhammer slipped and plunged into Iceman's hip. Chunks of flesh floated to the surface. The jackhammer slipped again and blasted apart Iceman's hip. Bits of battered bone splattered into the slushy soup.

An hour later the jackhammer ran out of compressed air. The body was still stuck in the glacier's icy grip. Frustrated, Koler radioed the helicopter to get him. He'd have to return another day. Koler's experience told him this was probably not a crime scene. If it was, then it happened a long time ago—probably decades, maybe more. Still, Koler shot a number of photos. He grabbed the ax in case it was evidence of foul play and headed to the landing area to meet the chopper.

At the station Koler's commander examined the ax. With a key he scratched the dull brown outer coat to reveal a bright orange metal underneath. *Copper,* he thought. Could this have been a murder weapon? He lined a box with newspaper, placed the ax inside, and stored it in the air-raid shelter.

September 22, 1991

The newspaper quoted Reinhold Messner, a world-famous mountain climber who had seen more than one accident victim in these mountains, as saying: "I consider it likely that the cadaver may be that of a prisoner of about 500 years ago. Masculine sex. I say prisoner because on the back there are perfectly visible some wounds that look like brands."

Local businessmen looked forward to the media attention that trailed behind the popular Messner, but this Iceman wasn't bringing the right kind of publicity. "Dead hiker trapped in ice" doesn't pack in tourists seeking an outdoor experience. The locals wanted the body out of there—the sooner the better.

A tavern owner and his friend took it upon themselves to expedite Iceman's removal. They hacked at the ice around the lower half of Iceman's body. For two hours they swung their picks. The pointed tools shredded Iceman's leggings. The men yanked Iceman's legs, trying to wrench him free. They pulled and tugged, but Iceman wouldn't let go. His right arm reached like an anchor line into solid ice.

Exhausted, the two called it a day and loaded a trash bag with the chunks of wood, string, leather, and fur they had dislodged while trying to free Iceman. The tavern owner thought he might use the bits and pieces to build a diorama showing what life had been like in the Alps centuries ago. Once back at the tavern, he called the police, telling them that the body was ready for recovery.

A BODY ON THE GLACIER: IS IT FROM 5 CENTURIES AGO?
—Alto Adige

September 23, 1991

The police officer on air-rescue duty that day and Rainer Henn, the director of forensic medicine at the University of Innsbruck, prepared the helicopter for a high-altitude landing. Thinking that the body had been dug out, the officer removed the shovel and ice pick to lighten the load. The thinner the air, the less lift rotor blades generate—every ounce counts.

Expecting a speedy removal, Henn arrived at the site without hat or gloves, his white hair blowing in the wind. He wasn't pleased when he saw a news team with camera rolling waiting for him. Reinhold Messner had started a buzz with his theories about Iceman. The reporter wanted answers from the professor: Just how old was Iceman? Could he really be from five centuries ago? The reporter peppered the forensic director with questions. But unlike the mountain climber, Henn wasn't going to make wild guesses. He wouldn't speculate. Henn looked to science for his answers.

One of the most difficult parts of Henn's job was to identify bodies that had been exposed to the elements for any length of time. It occurred to Henn that he could use the media to offer hikers some advice.

"It would be nice to [find] an identification card, passport, or an engraved wedding ring. For future mountain hikers, remember always to take these things with you to make the work of the forensic doctors easier."

Henn turned his back on the reporter and his questions. He wanted to get the job done and return to his warm office. Henn tried to lift the body, but the Iceman was still stuck.

"Do we have a pick?" Henn asked.

A hiker offered his ski pole and ice pick to the recovery team. The officer used the pick to chip at the ice, while Henn swept the slush away from the body as best he could with the ski pole.

The officer wedged the pick under Iceman and tried to pry him out of the ice. The frozen upper body bobbed on the end of the pick as the officer bounced on the handle. Iceman's lower body wouldn't budge. The officer let go of the pick, and Iceman's rigid torso smacked back against the ice.

Henn and the officer hacked and swept, struggling to cut around the lower body. When one section filled with ice chips and debris, the officer would move to another section, giving Henn room to sweep it clear. Now and again they stepped on Iceman's back as they climbed over him to switch positions.

Henn's ski pole struck a clump of hay.

"Look, it's straw," someone pointed out. "It's woven, look. There are strings."

When Henn and the officer finally freed Iceman, they rolled him onto his back. For the first time they all got a good look at the corpse's face. Shouldering his video camera, the cameraman zoomed in, while a photographer clicked away. Iceman, eyes wide open, stared right back and smiled a full-toothed grin for the cameras. His frozen and unyielding arms stretched straight out to his left, as if he were caught in a bizarre dance pose.

Henn and the police officer each took an end, lifted Iceman, and put him into a clear body bag. After moving the body bag out of the way, they turned their attention to the gravesite in order to, as Henn put it, "get a little bit for the archaeologists." Together they plunged bare hands into the meltwater, fishing out pieces of Iceman's leggings.

Henn poked around the boulders with the ski pole, looking for anything that might belong to Iceman. The officer joined him, turning over the area with the pick. It was hard to see into the inky water. When they cried out, the cameraman pivoted. He zoomed in on what they had discovered—a stone knife with a wooden handle. The cameraman panned the shot, settling on the ice pick. A hunk of hair dangled from the tip, then fell into the water.

With deadlines looming, the newsmen packed up their gear and boarded their helicopter. Henn, feeling the bitter cold, was eager to leave as well, but first he tried to pull a long whittled stick out of the ice. The hiker who had offered the pick and pole took hold of the stick with both hands and pulled. The wood sheered off at ice level with a loud crack. Henn tossed it, along with the stone knife and scraps of leather, into the body bag with Iceman. They'd been in this frigid pass for more than an hour. It was time to leave. The officer dragged the body bag, climbing over boulders on his way to the helicopter, while Henn trudged behind.

They flew to a nearby landing pad where an undertaker waited with a plain pine box for Iceman. When they tried to lay him in the coffin, he didn't fit. His arms, still frozen and sticking straight to the left, stuck out over the edge of the box. They had to force both arms into the coffin before they could close the lid.

By 4:00 that afternoon, Iceman was stretched out on a stainless-steel autopsy table in a small dissecting room at the Institute of Forensic Medicine in Innsbruck. A medical examiner studied the corpse. The body was not completely dehydrated. Totally dehydrated corpses are brittle and feather-light. This one had some give to it and didn't break when manipulated.

The body was naked except for the right foot. It looked like a bird's nest had been tied to Iceman's foot with string and leather. The medical examiner looked closer. Was this a shoe?

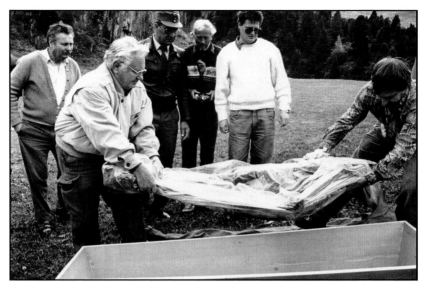

Before anybody realized the great antiquity and scientific importance of Iceman, he was treated like any other body found outdoors; he was placed in a body bag for transportation to the local morgue.

The medical examiner went through Iceman's belongings, looking for some form of identification. The ax looked old. The knife, too. Who was this man? Turning on his tape recorder, the doctor began his examination.

"Looks like an old mummy. Probable male. Weighs 55 pounds, give or take 10. No body hair left. No fingernails. No toenails. Recent damage to the left hip, leg and buttock . . . probable scavengers. Skeleton clearly visible."

The medical examiner rinsed grit off Iceman, all the while checking for wounds that might explain the cause of death. On Iceman's back, he noticed the markings that Messner had called brands. The short vertical lines were in groups, like four small bar codes, one on top of the other. Into the recorder he dictated, "From top to bottom there is first a group of four then in close proximity two groups of three, and lastly, barely visible, another group of four."

The medical examiner found more skin discolorations, which he referred to as tattoos—a cross on the inside of the right knee, a bracelet of parallel lines around the left wrist, and another group of vertical lines on the outside of the right ankle.

The glacier had contorted Iceman's right arm, wedging it permanently under his chin and straight off to the left. His fingers were "curved as if in a position for holding a round object." Curled fingers are common in corpses, but that was the only thing about this body that was ordinary. The medical examiner knew, without a doubt, that this body was meant for archaeologists.

September 24, 1991

For years archaeologist Konrad Spindler remembered the exact time the medical examiner pulled back the sheets covering Iceman. It was 8:05 in the morning.

When Spindler first entered the dissecting room, he was struck by the strong hospital smell. *Disinfectant,* he guessed, *perhaps phenol.* After a round of introductions and handshakes, Spindler turned his attention to the row of stainless-steel-topped slabs. It was so quiet he could hear the steady tick-tick of a clock marking time in the pale green room. Henn gave the signal to remove the sheet.

Spindler took one look at the corpse and another at the ax and then said without hesitation, "Roughly four thousand years old."

But he was already thinking,
Probably older.

Deductions
Iceman

In a blink the story of the glacier corpse's discovery flipped from mild local interest to global front-page frenzy. Iceman was the world's oldest mummified human. He was priceless. And he was rotting.

Defrosted and laid out in an autopsy room, Iceman showed worrisome signs. Black splotches were spreading over his skin. Was Iceman getting moldy? Decaying? Preservation became top priority.

Archaeologist Konrad Spindler took charge.

Spindler called Europe's best preservation workshop. The German scholars there eagerly agreed to restore Iceman's belongings, but refused to take the corpse. They had never worked on human remains. They had no advice for Spindler.

Scientists from all over the world offered opinions about how Iceman should be preserved, everything from fast-freezing him with nitroglycerin to cutting him up and storing his various parts in jars filled with formaldehyde. Archaeologists were used to working with skeletal remains, not with things that rot. Flesh and hair and organs—this wasn't familiar territory.

The director of the University of Innsbruck's Institute of Anatomy recommended mimicking the glacial conditions that had done such a wonderful job of preserving Iceman for thousands of years. Yet everyone worried that refreezing the body might cause damage. Thawing and refreezing tears tissue.

But it was their best shot, and they had to take it immediately.

Spindler and his colleagues blanketed Iceman in surgical gauze and placed him on a stretcher outfitted with a custom-fitted foam pad. They packed him in sterile crushed ice and covered the ice with a sterile plastic sheet. Then, as if they were building a layer cake, they piled on another layer.

The team placed the Iceman package into a freezer where the temperature and humidity were precisely maintained. Iceman's body rested on top of an electronic scale so that scientists could keep track of the slightest change in his weight. They installed alarms, prepared a backup chamber in case of a systems failure, and required an anatomy professor to carry a pager and be on call at all times in case of an Iceman emergency.

The Iceman Project was getting expensive—$10,000 per month, and that was just for storage. The research would run into tens of millions of dollars. Plans began for construction of a million-dollar facility just for Iceman.

Once the scientists were satisfied that Iceman's condition was stable, it was time to answer some burning questions.

What do we call him?

Naming an archaeological find is a science, and like most things scientific, there is a formula. A good name tells scholars important things about the find: where it was found, how old it is, *what* it is.

The formula for naming archaeological finds is: time period find belongs to + category of find + location of find (municipality) + nearest geographic designation + broad geographic location.

Iceman's official scientific name is: Late Neolithic glacier corpse from the Hauslabjock, Municipality Schnalls, Autonomous Province Bolzano/South Tyrol, Italy.

No one found this very catchy.

The French called the corpse Hibernatus after a horror movie where a man defrosts from the ice in the North Pole and miraculously comes back to life.

The Germans called the body Der Mann im Eis, "the man in the ice."

The irreverent Americans called him Frozen Fritz.

In the end the name that stuck was Ötzi. A journalist looking for an endearing spin on Iceman combined the words *Ötztal* (the nearby mountain range) and *yeti* (an abominable snowman). "This desiccated, horrible corpse must be made more positive, more charming if it's going to be a good story," the journalist said. "Ötzi" did the trick.

Now that Iceman had a name, the next pressing question was:

Just how old is Ötzi?

Until Konrad Spindler looked at Ötzi and his ax and guessed 4,000 years, everyone had assumed that Ötzi was from their century or at least from their millennium. The idea that this was the perfectly preserved corpse of a prehistoric man boggled the mind. Naturally, people wanted to know exactly when Ötzi lived.

Forensic experts working on Ötzi took samples for a carbon-14 dating test. They were just as judicious as Chatters had been when selecting the least destructive sample from Kennewick Man. They chose to remove bits of bone and fibers of tissue from his already-damaged left hip. To be absolutely certain that the items found with Ötzi (the ax, knife, bow, arrows, and clothing) belonged to him, they took a few blades of grass from Ötzi's woven cape. The bits from the body went to labs in Britain and Switzerland. Plant samples went to labs in Sweden and France. The test results came back. Ötzi was older than anyone had imagined. He was nearly 5,300 years old.

Does Ötzi belong to Austria or Italy?

Now aware of the importance of the body, officials returned to their maps. Originally the police had believed that the body lay in Austria. That was no longer agreed upon. An archaeological find belongs to the country where it is discovered, and a find like this is coveted. Could Ötzi have died inside Italy's border? Geographers were summoned. The surveyors measured.

Ötzi's gully lay in Italy—a mere 100 yards inside the border. Ötzi belonged to the Italians.

But local Italian officials were unprepared to take on the restoration of the artifacts. They didn't have the facilities to preserve the corpse. So, reluctantly and without giving up their claim to Ötzi, the Italians allowed the Austrians to continue their research—for the time being.

The Austrian archaeologists returned to Ötzi's gully in the summer of 1992. The trench, shaped like a ship's hull, was buried in snow. Worried that exhaust fumes might contaminate the site, the team dug by hand rather than use diesel machinery to get down to the layer they intended to study.

Working in the thin air of high altitude, a crew shoveled for three weeks, carrying away 600 tons of snow. They melted the last layer of ice with hair dryers. Their meticulous efforts were rewarded. In addition to pieces of Ötzi's clothing and his bearskin hat, they found pieces of Ötzi. Skin, muscle fibers, blood vessels, human hair, and even one fingernail were caught in the thin mesh of their sieves.

After five weeks of collecting 400 samples and hundreds of pounds of muck from the bottom of the gully, the crew packed up and headed for the lab, where the investigation would continue.

Body language

Everyone wanted a piece of Ötzi. The freezer door had barely clicked shut on him when the requests poured in, all requiring a sample of hair, skin, bone, or organ for research. There wasn't nearly enough Ötzi to go around. At the University of Innsbruck, they started with noninvasive tests.

Taking Ötzi's measurements wasn't as simple as pulling out a scale and a measuring tape. In his dehydrated state, he had shrunk to about 30 pounds. The biologists knew that 70 percent of a person's weight is water, and Ötzi had lost most of his. To determine how much Ötzi would have weighed, they calculated how much water he had lost. And to estimate Ötzi's height they measured something that doesn't shrink—his thighbone, which is the longest bone in the body and represents about a quarter of person's height. They calculated that Ötzi had weighed 110 pounds and had stood a little over five feet two inches at the time of his death.

Ötzi's fingernail proved that he had been seriously ill three times in the six months before he died. When the immune system is distressed, nails stop growing. After recovery the nail grows again, but not without leaving evidence. A ghostly line across the fingernail marks the stop-start place. Ötzi had three lines. The last line shows his most serious illness. Two months before he died, Ötzi had experienced a tough two weeks.

So how healthy was Ötzi when he died? He'd seen better days. His teeth were worn from chewing dried meat and the grit that gets into grain when it is milled on a grinding stone.

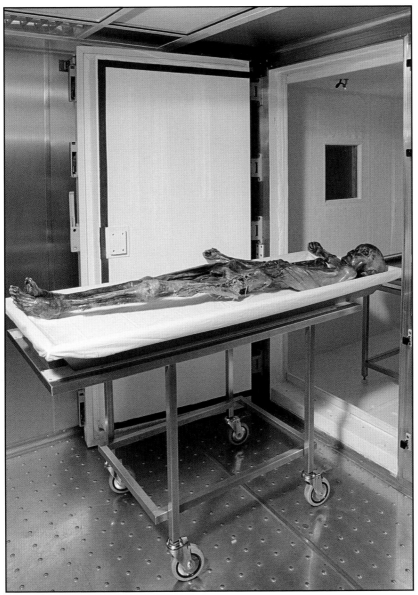

Ötzi is wheeled from his sterile, temperature-controlled storage room. He is rarely taken from his room, and then only for short periods. Scientists take special care to preserve Ötzi for future scientists.

And yet he was seriously undernourished, without an ounce of spare fat to insulate him against the high altitude's deadly cold. His arteries were clogged, and he had arthritis. The little toe on his left foot showed signs of repeated frostbite, the last bout just six months before his death. Campfires had blackened his lungs. His hair contained traces of arsenic and copper from working around copper smelting. He'd suffered broken ribs and a stroke. His intestines were infested with parasites. Ötzi was no stranger to pain.

The studies . . .

Klaus Oeggl, at the University of Innsbruck's Institute of Botany, was one of the lucky few to get a piece of Ötzi. "I got an amazing small amount of sample . . . the size of . . . the fingernail of the small finger." With that tiny sample from inside Ötzi's colon and the material collected from the site, Oeggl hoped to reconstruct an entire prehistoric environment.

Oeggl had been working on the Iceman Project for some time. He and his students had been picking through the hundreds of pounds of sludge retrieved from Ötzi's gully. Armed with tiny tweezers, they picked botanical bits out of the mounds of mud. They sorted grass from hair, twigs from twine. Their backs ached from long days of peering at these samples through microscopes.

When Oeggl received the precious sample from Ötzi's colon, he thought about how best to extract from it everything there was to know about Ötzi's last meal. Oeggl decided to cut the sample into four parts. One part he would save unaltered, and the other three he would use for tests involving chemicals. Oeggl removed a piece of Ötzi from the freezer and began his investigation. First he added a few drops of

The tavern owner recovered only a portion of Ötzi's belongings. An archaeological team works the site searching for anything that once belonged to Ötzi. They hope to rescue all that remains before exposure and meltwater destroy his fragile possessions.

saline solution to plump the sample. Once it was rehydrated, he took a look at it under an electron microscope.

A blizzard of snowflake-like cell patterns appeared, which Oeggl recognized immediately as a primitive form of wheat called einkorn. The wheat had been farmed. Ötzi had been connected to a farming community.

Through the microscope Oeggl could see that the skins of the wheat grains were broken. The wheat had been ground into flour. *Probably for making bread,* he thought. Oeggl increased the magnification. He noticed black speckles on the grains—charcoal from burned evergreens. The bread had been baked over an open fire.

A botanist can be an exceptional detective. If Ötzi had walked through a grass field, Oeggl would have known it. If Ötzi had leaned up against a pine tree, Oeggl would have known it. It would all be there in his intestines. The pollens would prove it.

Oeggl was anxious to find out which pollens were in Ötzi's intestines. But first he had to destroy part of one of the samples—something he hated to do. To get a good look at the pollen grains, he needed to dissolve the fats and proteins that were obscuring them. The question was how. Which chemical would do the least damage? Alcohol, he decided.

Oeggl took a deep breath and applied alcohol to the sample—once, twice. He increased the magnification. There, through the lens, he spotted pollen. There are more than 700 possible types of pollen that Ötzi could have come in contact with, and Oeggl knew them all by heart. But the one floating before his eyes wasn't one he had expected to see. It wasn't *which* pollen the plant had come from that surprised Oeggl, but *when*.

Everyone had assumed that Ötzi had died in autumn, and that winter snows had buried him immediately, hiding his body from predators. The pollen Oeggl was looking at came from a flower that blossomed between March and June. Oeggl said, "The pollen was consumed immediately after the flowering of the plant . . . which means that the Iceman died in spring and not in autumn, as it was presumed before."

Oeggl ran DNA studies on the food remnants. Breakage is a problem when collecting new DNA strands; ancient strands are even more troublesome. But Oeggl was able to identify wild goat, red deer, and several mosses. Since there was no

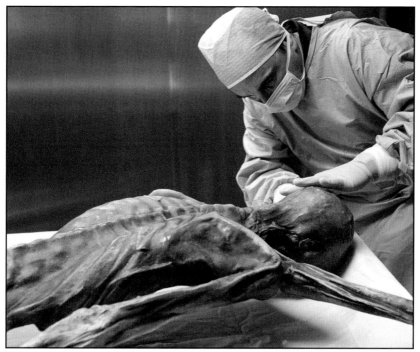

Scholars dress as if they are surgeons headed to the operating room in order to prevent contaminating Ötzi when they examine him.

evidence that prehistoric people had actually eaten moss, Oeggl deduced that Ötzi had wrapped his food in moss to keep it fresh—prehistoric plastic wrap.

The fingernail-sized sample from the intestines allowed Oeggl to map Ötzi's final journey. Ötzi had walked through a woody evergreen area, stopping to eat some wild goat, bread, and vegetables. Then he climbed above the tree line and dined on red deer.

Ötzi's body revealed not only his last journey, but also the places he had traveled throughout his life. What we eat eventually makes its way into our bones and teeth. Earth scientists took soil and water samples from all over the Alps and compared them to what was in Ötzi's bones and teeth. When they found a match, the scientists knew where Ötzi had been. The team studying Ötzi's movements believed his travels were limited to valleys within 50 miles of where he died.

Artifacts

Unlike Lapedo Child, no one prepared Ötzi's body for burial. No one dressed him in special clothes or planted special grave goods with him. He came to us as if delivered by a time machine—dressed in his everyday clothes, carrying the gear a prehistoric man might.

The glacier preserved what prehistorians consider priceless treasures—clothing, feathered arrows, birch-bark containers. Most often, scholars have to be satisfied cobbling together a picture of Neolithic life from bits of pottery, bones and teeth, flint tools, and arrowheads. Organic possessions disintegrate.

Many of Ötzi's belongings had been damaged during the recovery. His bow had been snapped in two. One of his birch-bark containers had been stepped on and crushed. The dagger and its scabbard had been struck by an ice pick. His clothing had been reduced to scraps. It was a lot of work to put it all back together again.

Archaeologist Markus Egg was in charge of restoring Ötzi's clothes and belongings. The Roman-Germanic Central Museum in Germany where Egg worked was known for its restoration recipes. Even though the museum officials had to refuse the corpse itself, they were excited about the prospect of working on the artifacts—the museum's specialty.

Egg's first task was to inspect, catalog, and make detailed records of the artifacts. They were photographed, x-rayed, sketched, described in detail, and scanned for three-dimensional computer imaging. Egg's team filled notebook after notebook after notebook.

When the inventory was complete, the team took samples before the artifacts were contaminated by the chemicals used to preserve them. The researchers stored the uncontaminated bits so they would be able to refer back to the artifacts in their original condition if need be.

Next the artifacts were cleaned in distilled water. The dirty water was strained through fine mesh and filters to capture every particle.

Each material had its own restoration recipe. Grasses were soaked in chemicals inside a vacuum chamber and then dried by freezing. Fur was soaked in a grease mixture and then dried *before* freezing. Wood sat in a bath of deionized water for months, and then the restorers kept careful watch while the wood slowly air-dried. They were careful not to let the wood crack or split from overdrying or drying too quickly.

Once the materials were clean and stable, the restorers moved to the next phase in the Iceman Project—to reassemble all the pieces and figure out what Ötzi was wearing and what he was carrying with him.

Ötzi gets dressed

The expert working on the leather pieces had soaked them in a fatty concoction to restore their suppleness and freeze-dried them to remove excess water. While handling the pieces, she noticed an animal-like odor coming from the leather. She wondered, *Am I smelling Ötzi?*

She arranged the scraps of leather according to color, using the seams as a starting point, as we might use the straight line of a puzzle's outer edge. Piece by piece she

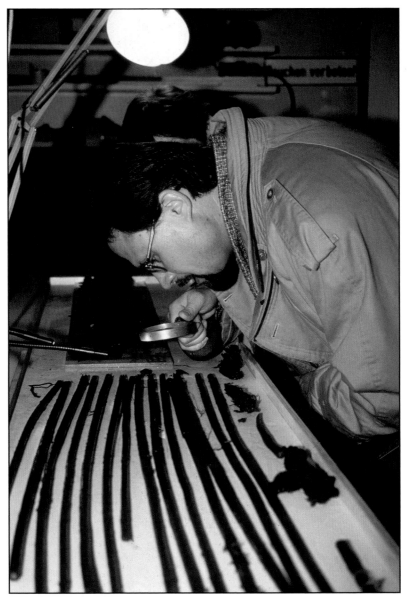

Dr. Klaus Oeggl examines Otzi's arrows.

assembled the garments until a picture of Ötzi's wardrobe came together.

Bum bag

British skiers call it a bum bag; American shoppers call it a fanny pack. We don't know what Ötzi called it, but he wore the prehistoric version—a pouch on a belt worn around the waist. Ötzi most likely wore his pouch in the front under his clothing to keep the contents dry, and he used his as a tool case. In the pouch he stored a bone with two pointed ends for punching tiny holes in leather when sewing, a scraper to clean animal skins, a drilling tool, a carving tool, and tinder for lighting fires.

Loincloth

Ötzi's loincloth was made from three-foot strips of leather whipstitched together with sinew—thread made from animal muscles and tendons. The scarf-shaped piece of leather was still wrinkled from where it had bunched between Ötzi's legs.

Leggings

Imagine thigh-high boots without feet. That's how Ötzi kept his legs warm. He held the leggings up with straps that may have attached to his bum-bag belt. Ötzi's leggings were cleverly designed. They had tongue-shaped pieces that covered the tops of his feet and kept his leggings securely tucked into his boots.

Fur coat

Too many pieces of Ötzi's fur coat were missing for the restorers to tell if it had had sleeves or a collar. The coat was striped, made by alternating strips of light and dark fur. It wasn't clear if Ötzi had draped it over his shoulders or if it had had arm holes. But the restorers could tell it had been the size and shape of an enormous bath sheet, and it would have reached below his knees.

Grass cape

Ötzi wore a cape made from long bunches of grass that hung straight down with their roots still attached. The grass was held together by strands that were twisted and braided horizontally around the cape. The ends were left to hang free below the hip, like fringe, so that Ötzi could walk and climb with ease. The grass cape was Ötzi's waterproof layer—his raincoat. He wore it over his clothes.

Birch-bark tube

Ötzi carried a birch-bark tube in which he stored embers, wrapped in fresh maple leaves, for making a fire. The tube was found near Ötzi's outstretched hand, warped, brittle, and broken. After treating it with steam, the restorers were able to bend it back into its original cylindrical shape.

Dagger

A dagger has two cutting edges. A knife has one sharp edge. Ötzi's dagger was so small that if it hadn't had its handle attached, the restorers probably would have called it an arrowhead. Archaeologists may have to rethink small flint blades they've found elsewhere and labeled arrowheads—perhaps these were once daggers, too.

Ax

Ötzi's ax may have been his most prized possession. The blade was made by pouring molten copper into a mold. The

This reconstruction, displayed at the Museum of Archaeology in Italy, shows what scientists believe Ötzi wore on that fatal day in the Alps more than 5,000 years ago.

handle came from the nook of a yew trunk to make what scholars call a knee-joint shaft. The branch stub was split like a fork to sandwich the copper blade in place, and then the blade was cemented to the handle with a layer of birch pitch— prehistoric superglue. To make the connection even more secure, narrow leather strips were tightly wound around the joint.

What scholars don't know is if Ötzi ever used his ax. Copper is very soft. It doesn't make a good chopping tool. Could his ax have carried some symbolic meaning? And if it was more than a tool or a weapon, what did it mean to Ötzi?

Quiver of arrows

When it was recovered, Ötzi's fur quiver looked more like a leather sack—the only hairs that remained were those snagged in the seams. In addition to arrows, Ötzi stored antler fragments for points and a coiled string in the quiver. The restorers decided not to unwind the string. That act would be irreversible. As science progresses, so do scientific tests. It's best to leave as much of Ötzi and his things as possible for future generations to explore. Tomorrow's scholars will be able to learn things in ways today's scholars have yet to imagine.

Medicine

Ötzi carried two fungal growths that looked like mushrooms. This fungus is often found at the base of old birch trees. Until the beginning of the 20th century, it was used to treat all kinds of diseases. Scholars believe that Ötzi knew about its healing properties.

Marble

One of Ötzi's possessions had scholars scratching their heads.

It was a tassel of sinew threaded through a hole in a button-shaped, brilliant-white piece of marble. Was it a magic charm? Protection against evil spirits? A piece of jewelry? Or was it just a convenient way to carry repair thread, keeping it from tangling by threading it through a buttonhole?

✦ ✦ ✦

Ötzi's belongings currently fill glass cases in a building befitting such priceless artifacts—a former bank turned museum in Bolzano, Italy. Now restored and stable, these artifacts offer museum visitors a snapshot of Copper Age humans.

How did Ötzi die?

Despite all the examinations, studies, computer analyses, and endless hypothesizing, it was 10 years before scientists unlocked the mystery of Ötzi's death. And it had been right in front of them the whole time.

In 1998, surrounded by bodyguards and swarmed by paparazzi, Ötzi was transferred to the museum in Bolzano, where he went on display. Once he was moved, he was not often taken from the safety of his high-tech, sterile, climate-controlled chamber. Most requests to study Ötzi were denied.

In 2001, after months of consideration, Ötzi's official caretaker, pathologist Eduard Egarter Vigl, approved one study. Egarter Vigl prepared to remove a sliver of bone from Ötzi's broken right rib. The bone fragment was to be used in a study to determine if the break occurred before Ötzi died or after. Egarter Vigl wanted to know the precise location of the fracture before he cut into Ötzi's chest to extract bone. He ordered a complete series of chest x-rays.

The x-rays revealed an odd triangular shape. Was this a

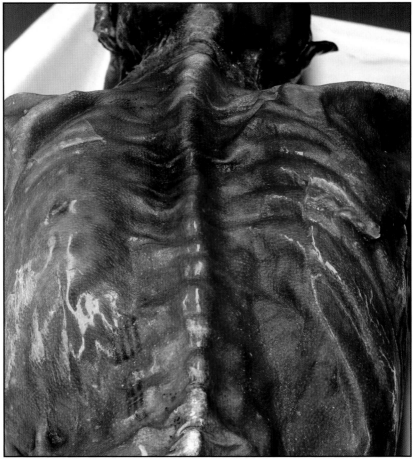

Groups of bar tattoos on Ötzi's back may have been decorative or part of a healing ritual performed to relieve pain. The wound above and to the left of the tattoos is the entry point of the arrowhead that triggered speculation that Iceman had been murdered.

blemish on the film? A computer error? They compared the new x-rays to an old set. The triangle appeared in the old x-rays, too. How had everyone missed this? The triangular mass was five times denser than bone. It was a flint arrowhead lodged in Ötzi's shoulder.

Dressed in sterile scrubs, Egarter Vigl opened the insulated door to Ötzi's chamber. After entering the cold, brightly lit antechamber, he stepped through a second door and into the inner rooms where Ötzi was kept in a display vault. Egarter Vigl slid Ötzi onto a gurney and rolled him into an examining room. Using the heat from his hands, he defrosted the icy glaze that coated and protected Ötzi's skin. Sure enough, Egarter Vigl found an entrance wound on Ötzi's left shoulder. He could see a narrow channel where something had pierced skin and muscle on its way to the shoulder blade.

Later Egarter Vigl found cuts on Ötzi's right hand. Discoloration around the cuts indicated Ötzi had been alive when he was wounded. He'd bled. Egarter Vigl said, "I think that the wound was very painful. Two fingers are nearly immobilized." It looked as if Ötzi hadn't died from cold and hunger, as the early theories claimed. Ötzi had been shot in the back.

We will never know who killed Ötzi and why, but his body is helping answer other mysteries. Breakthroughs in genetic research can show us where he, and those who came before him, lived. Population studies are using genetics to map the movements of our ancestors. It won't be long before genetic markers will be the GPS of human prehistory. But like every road, it's one with its share of roadblocks, as scientists who were studying Iceman and other hominins discovered.

Debates
Iceman

At the Institute of Molecular Medicine at Oxford University in Great Britain, geneticist Bryan Sykes had developed a method for recovering DNA from ancient bones. Members of the Iceman Project contacted Sykes to see if he would be willing to try his method on Iceman. Sykes had never attempted an extraction from remains this ancient, but he believed his chances were good. Protected over the millennia by glacier ice, Iceman's remains were kept beyond the reach of the water and oxygen that would have destroyed his DNA.

The Iceman Project provided Sykes with material for his extraction process. In his book *The Seven Daughters of Eve,* Sykes wrote, "It looked awfully unremarkable, a sort of gray mush. When I opened the jar and started to pick through the contents with a pair of forceps it seemed to be a mixture of skin and fragments of bone."

From that unremarkable gray mush, Sykes recovered Iceman's 5,300-year-old DNA. Sykes ran tests on Iceman's DNA, comparing it to his own database, a collection of DNA samples taken from people currently living all over Europe. To his astonishment Iceman's DNA precisely matched one of the samples. Iceman had a descendant working in Sykes's own lab!

Sykes was convinced that the connection he had discovered between Iceman and Europeans today was just the first step in resolving many of the major debates about the human past. He believed our mtDNA held road maps of when and what populations moved around the globe. Sykes said that "individuals today were as reliable a witness to past events as any bronze dagger or piece of pottery." With those words Sykes opened the door for disagreement. Nothing ignites debates like the introduction of a new technology.

Sykes examined the spread of farming in prehistoric Europe. Domestication of crops and animals began about 10,000 BCE in southwest Asia in a region that scientists call the Fertile Crescent. This area spans modern-day Syria, Jordan, Lebanon, Israel, Egypt, Iraq, Turkey, and Iran. Hunter-gatherers in the Fertile Crescent were the first to make the transition from food collector to food producer. They were the first to discover that the seeds from wild grasses that they had foraged could be planted and harvested in a predictable fashion. Agriculture was born.

Farming spread across Europe. One of the many disagreements among scientists about farming is *how* it spread. Did the concept of farming spread as local hunter-gatherer populations began to plant seeds? Or did the farmers themselves spread and overwhelm local hunter-gatherers?

Until the 1970s the theory in vogue was that the hunter-gatherers who occupied Europe slowly adopted farming methods. There was no mad dash of farmers from southwest Asia.

That all changed in 1971, when geneticist Luigi Luca Cavalli-Sforza presented a theory he called demic diffusion (people migration). Cavalli-Sforza believed it was the farmers who colonized Europe, bringing their knowledge with them. Demic diffusion proposed that southwest Asian farmers nudged European hunter-gatherers out of their habitat in a slow but steady advance. Cavalli-Sforza calculated how fast the farmers had spread by using radiocarbon dates from agricultural sites, and he proposed a speed of expansion of about one kilometer a year, depending on the region.

Over the years the theory was distorted by those who took to calling the diffusion a "wave of advance." This variation on Cavalli-Sforza's theory imagines a veritable tidal wave of sickle-waving farmers storming fertile ground and wiping out any hunter-gatherer daring to stand his ground. Most scientists were in agreement that southwest Asian farmers had replaced hunter-gatherers; the debate became how fast this had happened.

Demic diffusion was the favored theory when Sykes made his genetic discoveries using Iceman's DNA. Sykes's research pointed in an entirely different direction. Modern European DNA was not tracking back to farmers in southwest Asia, as it should if there had been a large-scale migration. Modern Europeans appeared to be descendants of the indigenous hunter-gatherers. Genetics was saying farming, not farmers, spread from southwest Asia. Iceman had started trouble.

Conferences are where scientists come together to share new findings. In *The Seven Daughters of Eve,* Sykes described his experience at the Second Euroconference on Population History, held in 1995, where he took on demic diffusion and its champions. His 20-minute presentation got off to a rocky start when his introducer, Sir Walter Bodmer, dismissed him before he even began, saying, "And the next speaker is Bryan Sykes, who is talking about mitochondria. I don't believe in mitochondria."

At the podium Sykes was distracted by Cavalli-Sforza and Bodmer, who didn't try to hide their disdain. Sykes's speech was punctuated by their cries of "rubbish" and "nonsense" in ever-increasing decibels. Sykes wrote, "As I came to the concluding slide, I could almost see the steam coming out of their ears." Sykes expected fireworks, and he got them.

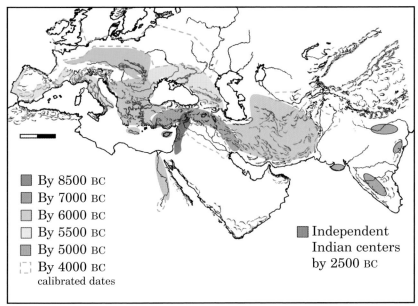

By 8500 BC
By 7000 BC
By 6000 BC
By 5500 BC
By 5000 BC
By 4000 BC
calibrated dates

Independent
Indian centers
by 2500 BC

This map, based on archaeological discoveries, shows that agriculture spread around the Mediterranean Sea and northwest across Europe after the first domestication of crops in southwest Asia.

Bodmer and Cavalli-Sforza pelted Sykes with questions designed to shred his theory. The debate became so heated that it took an odd turn. Bodmer claimed that he and Cavalli-Sforza had never suggested that an influx of farmers from southwest Asia had replaced the hunter-gatherers. In a show-stopping move, Sykes read from a textbook that Bodmer and Cavalli-Sforza had coauthored. Given that the page had been marked with a bright yellow adhesive note, Sykes must have expected the denial and prepared for it. When Bodmer heard in his own words the scenario for replacement, he sat down in a huff. But the debate didn't end there.

Overturning popular opinion isn't something that is done quietly. Scientists don't willingly let go of theories they've spent years, often decades, formulating. The intense examination, though, can actually be healthy. Debates are useful for uncovering flaws in a theory.

Demic diffusion followers' next move was to attack the method. Mutterings in the scientific community targeted mtDNA. The strands were too short. The mutation rates were off. The samples were misleading.

In the end mtDNA stood up to the attacks. Today the popularity of demic diffusion is waning. Most scholars believe the debate isn't as simple as the spread of farmers versus the spread of farming practices. Archaeology and genetics are unveiling a complex combination of factors that initiated agriculture and its spread around the world.

New studies in genetics, such as looking at generations of Y chromosomes in nuclear DNA, have spawned theories of men traveling as the Iceman did—male farmers trekking into Europe and marrying indigenous female hunter-gatherers.

The groundbreaking extraction of DNA from Iceman is now a relatively routine procedure. As our scientific methods become refined, so will the explanations for prehistoric events. Genetics is the current celebrity of research methods, but one can't help but wonder what's next. One thing is certain: whatever it is, it won't escape the scrutiny of debate.

Further reading on Iceman

Fowler, Brenda. *Iceman: Uncovering the Life and Times of a Prehistoric Man Found in an Alpine Glacier.* Chicago: University of Chicago Press, 2000.

Spindler, Konrad. *The Man in the Ice: The Discovery of a 5,000-Year-Old Body Reveals the Secrets of the Stone Age.* New York: Harmony Books, 1994.

Websites

NOVA Online/Ice Mummies/The Iceman's Last Meal
http://www.pbs.org/wgbh/nova/icemummies/iceman.html
Nova looks at Iceman's last meal.

Oetzi, the Iceman
http://www.mummytombs.com/main.otzi.htm
Lots of information on Iceman and other mummies all over the world.

A Unique Find/Ötzi—South Tyrol Museum of Archaeology
http://www.archaeologiemuseum.it/en/oetzi-the-iceman
Iceman not only has his own museum, but also his own website.

Source notes (See Bibliography on p. 178 for full citations.)

"How could they spoil . . ." *Iceman,* p. 7.
"Look, it's a person. . . ." *Iceman,* p. 7.
"19th September 1991—Around 12:00 . . ." *The Man in the Ice,* p.13.
"I consider it likely that . . ." *Iceman,* p. 25.
"A BODY ON THE GLACIER . . ." *Iceman,* p. 25.
"It would be nice to . . ." *Iceman,* pp. 30–31.
"Do we have a pick?" *Iceman,* p. 30.
"Look, it's straw. . . ." *Iceman,* p. 31.
"get a little bit for . . ." *Iceman,* p. 31.
"Looks like an old mummy. . . ." *Iceman,* p. 35.
"From top to bottom there . . ." *The Man in the Ice,* p. 39.
"curved as if in a . . ." *Iceman,* p. 36.
"Roughly four thousand . . ." Roberts, David. "The Iceman Lone Voyager from the Copper Age." *National Geographic* 183 (6), June 1993.
"This desiccated, horrible corpse . . ." *The Man in the Ice,* p. 77.
"I got an amazing small . . ." BBC interview transcript:
http://www.bbc.co.uk/science/horizon/2001/icemantrans.shtml
"The pollen was consumed immediately . . ." BBC interview transcript:
http://www.bbc.co.uk/science/horizon/2001/icemantrans.shtml
"I think that the wound . . ." Cullen, Bob. "Testimony of the Iceman." *Smithsonian* magazine, February 2003, pp. 42–50.
"It looked awfully unremarkable. . . ." *The Seven Daughters of Eve,* p. 5.
"individuals today were as reliable . . ." *The Seven Daughters of Eve,* p. 8.
"And the next speaker is . . ." *The Seven Daughters of Eve,* p. 150.
"As I came to the . . ." *The Seven Daughters of Eve,* p. 151.

Conclusion

Video games and Hollywood have created images of archaeologists at work—dramatic images involving tomb raiding and bullwhips. Documentaries feature dusty scientists dressed in shorts and hiking boots in some remote location, unable to contain their excitement about a find. But the reality is that much of today's archaeological work is carried out in labs and universities. Months, years, even decades, may be dedicated to teasing a single secret about our past from data painstakingly collected and organized.

Archaeology, like all sciences, has become specialized. The sheer volume of information makes it impossible for any one person to keep up. Scholars are forced to narrow their focus. They dedicate careers to subjects that their early predecessors wouldn't have dreamed were significant—subjects such as tooth enamel. Yet Turkana Boy's teeth told us how old he was when he died. Lapedo Child's teeth told us about his childhood illnesses. And Iceman's teeth revealed where he spent his youth. Who knows what tomorrow's scientists will be able to deduce from these very same teeth?

If Lapedo Child had been discovered a few generations ago, there is no doubt that those bits of charcoal and grains of pollen would have been trampled underfoot in the rush to yank the boy's bones from his grave. And just a little over a decade ago, Iceman's belongings were hacked from the ice, with no regard to their location in respect to his body or the surrounding area. Once a find has been ripped from its findspot, there is no going back. No second chance to apply science's advancements.

Today's archaeologists understand that disturbance of a find's context may obliterate a piece of evidence crucial for some future discovery. They understand that the least-invasive methods preserve the most potential information. They understand the importance of preserving precious remains for future study.

The ability to answer questions improves along with scientific techniques and instruments. It's only in the past few years that high-resolution computer scans have proved that the arrow lodged in Iceman's collarbone nicked an artery, causing him to bleed to death. Until that technology was available, scholars debated whether he died in a fall, from his wounds, or from the cold.

Although advancements offer more-detailed information, they come with concerns. As archaeologists splinter off into highly specialized fields, their work is no longer about asking the big questions—Where did we come from? How did we get here? What was life like for our prehistoric ancestors? Their work is now so focused, it's as if the scholars are studying the forest by peering at the leaves.

Scientists spend years entrenched in their topic. But at some point, they are forced to step back. Usually this happens after they publish or when they present their work at a conference. This is when debates are most likely to erupt. That eye socket they'd studied for months suddenly explodes into a war over who populated the Americas. That peculiar jaw triggers a battle about what our ancestors did once they left Africa. That tiny strand of DNA fuels arguments on how farming began in Europe.

Given the fury of the debates, it's no wonder scientists are more comfortable working on the leaf and are leery about fitting it into the forest. And yet it's from a matchbook-sized scrap of skull, a pinhole in a periwinkle, the point of an arrow-head, and a fingernail-sized chunk of intestine that archaeolo-gists wheedle a three-dimensional picture of the past.

In the end those leaves answer questions about the forest. How did language evolve? Ethnicity? Agriculture? Each con-tribution takes us a step closer to understanding migration, adaptation, and invention along with endless universal ques-tions about human behavior and cultural organization. All this from meager evidence that has survived the millennia.

There is no doubt that the next generation will have far superior tools and techniques at their disposal. Turkana Boy, Lapedo Child, Kennewick Man, and Iceman will continue whispering their secrets into the ears of tomorrow's archaeol-ogists. Their stories have just begun.

Further reading

Archaeology
Bahn, Paul. *Written in the Bones: How Human Remains Unlock the Secrets of the Dead.* Toronto: Firefly Books, 2003.
Dillehay, Thomas D. *The Settlement of the Americas: A New Prehistory.* New York: Basic Books, 2000.
Morell, Virginia. *Ancestral Passions: The Leakey Family and the Quest for Humankind's Beginnings.* New York: Simon & Schuster, 1995.
Oakes, Ted. *Land of the Lost Monsters: Man Against Beast: The Prehistoric Battle for the Planet.* New York: Hydra Publishing, 2003.
Schick, Kathy D., and Nicholas Toth. *Making Silent Stones Speak: Human Evolution and the Dawn of Technology.* New York: Simon & Schuster, 1993.

Tracing human ancestry

Robertshaw, Peter and Jill Rubalcaba. *The Early Human World*. New York: Oxford University Press, 2004.

Sykes, Bryan. *The Seven Daughters of Eve*. New York: W. W. Norton & Company, 2001.

Tankersley, Kenneth B. *In Search of Ice Age Americans*. Salt Lake City: Gibbs Smith, 2002.

Archaeology and anthropology

Anthropology.net
    http://anthropology.net/
    Keep up with the latest breaking news in anthropology at this site.
Archaeology Magazine
    http://www.archaeology.org/
    Follow the latest news in archaeology.
ArchNet: Table of Contents for WWW Virtual Library for Archaeology
    http://archnet.asu.edu/toc/toc.php
    Find out what's happening in the lab and in the field.
Emuseum Main Page
    http://www.mnsu.edu/emuseum/index.shtml
    Minnesota State University's anthropology and archaeology museum.
Outpost: Human Origins @nationalgeographic.com
    http://www.nationalgeographic.com/outpost/
    See archaeologists at National Geographic outposts at work.
Prehistoric Life—What is a fossil?
    http://museumvictoria.com.au/prehistoric/what/index.html
    Museum Victoria shows how fossils are formed.

Human origins

Becoming Human
    http://www.becominghuman.org/
    Donald Johanson is your guide through this interactive documentary that tells the story of 4 million years of human evolution.
Evolution: Human Origins of Humankind
    http://www.pbs.org/wgbh/evolution/humans/humankind/k.html
    PBS shows sketches of specific hominin finds grouped by species.
The Human Origins Program at the Smithsonian Institution
    http://anthropology.si.edu/humanorigins/index2.htm
    Explores what makes us human in a journey through evolution.
San Diego Museum of Man—Footsteps Through Time
    http://www.abouthumanevolution.org/html/site/timestone11.htm
    Travel back 4 million years via this on-line exhibit.

Time Line

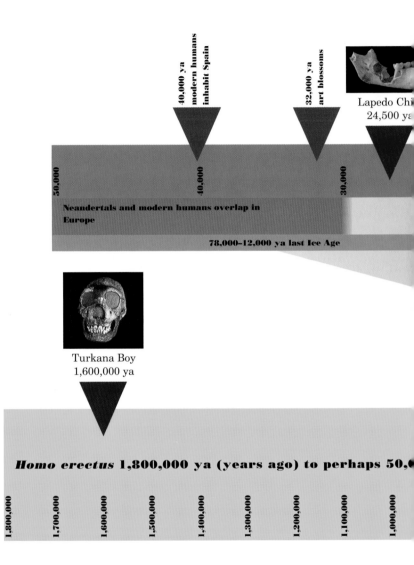

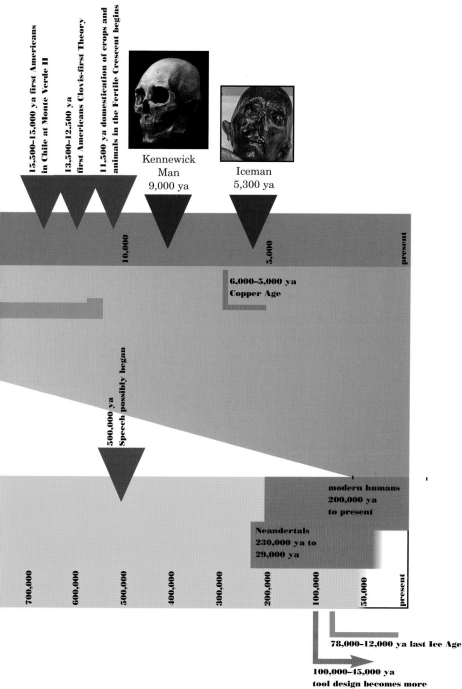

15,500–15,000 ya first Americans
in Chile at Monte Verde II

13,500–12,500 ya
first Americans Clovis-first Theory

11,500 ya domestication of crops and
animals in the Fertile Crescent begins

Kennewick
Man
9,000 ya

Iceman
5,300 ya

10,000

5,000

present

6,000–5,000 ya
Copper Age

500,000 ya
Speech possibly began

modern humans
200,000 ya
to present

Neandertals
230,000 ya to
29,000 ya

700,000 600,000 500,000 400,000 300,000 200,000 100,000 50,000 present

78,000–12,000 ya last Ice Age

100,000–45,000 ya
tool design becomes more
complicated and specialized

Glossary

acacia (uh-KAY-shuh) tree: A woody legume plant with feathery leaves and white or yellow flowers that is native to warm-temperate regions. Also known as a thorn tree.

acetone: A solvent for organic materials. It's also an ingredient in fingernail polish remover.

anthropologist: A person who studies the origins and behavior, as well as the cultural, physical, and social lives, of humans.

archaeologist: A person who studies historic and prehistoric peoples and their cultures by way of their remains (both fossils and artifacts).

archaeozoologist: A person who studies extinct and living animals by way of their remains.

artifact: An object made by humans.

backdirt: The loosened dirt created when excavating.

bioanthropologist: A person who studies the human species from an evolutionary perspective.

botanist: A person who studies plant life.

Broca's area: A section of the human brain involved in processing, producing, and comprehending speech.

browridge: A bony prominence above the eyes.

cadaver: A dead body.

cairn: A landmark made from a pile of stones.

calcium: A major chemical component of bone and shell.

carbon-12: A carbon atom.

carbon-14: A radioactive isotope of carbon, often used in dating objects.

carnivore: A meat-eating animal.

cartilage: Flexible, fibrous connective tissue.

centrifuge: A device that rotates at high speed to separate substances of differing densities.

chough (CHUFF): A kind of raven.

chromosome: A threadlike body of the cell nucleus that carries the genes in linear order.

clavicle: Collarbone.

Clovis-first theory: The idea that the first immigrants into the Americas were Siberian hunters traveling by land through an ice-free corridor at the end of the last Ice Age.

cobble: A rounded stone used to strike and flake another stone.

Copper Age: A period between the Stone and Bronze ages marked by the development of copper tools.

coprolites: Fossilized feces.

Cossacks: Militant people, primarily from southern Russia, who were known for their horsemanship.

cranium: The part of the skull that covers the brain.

CT scan, also CAT scan: CAT stands for computerized axial tomography, the method used to produce a three-dimensional image of a cross section of the body using a series of two-dimensional x-rays.

cytoplasm: The jellylike substance that makes up much of the cell inside the cell membrane.

deionize: To remove electrically charged particles called ions.

demic diffusion: The idea that a group of people spread into an area that was previously uninhabited by that group, possibly displacing, replacing, or interbreeding with the preexisting population.

DNA: A material found in the nucleus of a cell that carries the genetic information in all life forms.

einkorn (EYNE-korn): A primitive form of wheat.

en bloc removal: An excavation technique that minimizes disturbance by removing the earth around the object along with the object.

epiphyseal (ih-pih-FIH-see-ul) **fusion:** A closure formed at the end of arm and leg bones when growth is complete.

extant: Still existing.

extinct: No longer existing.

femur: The long bone from the hip to the knee; thighbone.

Fertile Crescent: An agricultural region in southwest Asia that was once fertile and is now part desert.

flake: To remove chips from a larger stone by hammering it with a fist-sized stone or cobble.

flint: A hard, fine-grained stone primarily used to start a fire.

formaldehyde: A solution used as a preservative or disinfectant.

fossil: Remains or traces of a living thing, such as a skeleton or footprint, that is embedded and preserved in the ground.

FOXP2: A gene related to language skills.

fungus (_plural:_ fungi): Any of a group of soft spongy plants without leaves or green parts. Mushrooms, mold, and mildew are all fungi.

geoarchaeologist: A person who studies the earth as it was in the past.

gene: A hereditary unit that occupies a specific place on a chromosome and determines a specific characteristic in a life form.

geneticist: A biologist who specializes in heredity.

genetics: A branch of biology that deals with heredity.

genome: All the inheritable traits of a life form.

grave wax: A waxy fat residue on decomposing material.

half-life: The time it takes for one half of the atoms in a given amount of a radioactive substance to decay.

Hominidae (haw-MIN-uh-dye): The family of mammals that includes modern humans and their extinct ancestors; also "hominid."

hominin: humans or a human ancestor.

Homo erectus: The first hominin species to leave Africa. *Homo erectus* lived 1.8 to 0.2 million years ago and is one of many ancestors of modern humans.

Homo neanderthalensis: A hominin species that inhabited Europe and parts of western and central Asia between circa 230,000 and 29,000 years ago; Neandertal.

hunter-gatherers: Hominins who collect food by hunting and foraging.

hybrid: Offspring produced by cross-breeding two unlike species.

Iberian Peninsula: A peninsula in southwestern Europe occupied by modern day Spain, Portugal, Andorra, Gibraltar, and the southwestern tip of France.

ilium: The broad area of spongy bone where the major muscles in the leg and back attach to the pelvis.

in situ: Situated in place, undisturbed.

Kikichwa (kee-keetch-wa): (Swahili) "The language of the skulls."

Lagar Velho: Meaning "old olive press" in Portuguese, Lagar Velho is a rock-shelter site in the Lapedo Valley of Portugal where the Lapedo Child was found.

larynx: The part of the trachea containing the vocal chords.

linguist: A person who studies languages.

lumbar vertebra: Part of the lower backbone

mitochondrial DNA (mtDNA): The genetic material located in the mitochondria of the cell.

mitochondrion (*plural:* mitochondria): The portion of the cell that produces energy.

multiregional theory: A theory of modern human origins that proposes modern humans evolved at the same time in more than one area.

mutation: A change in the DNA sequence.

NAGPRA (Native American Graves Protection and Repatriation Act): A federal law requiring that Native American cultural items and human remains be returned to their respective tribes.

Nariokotome (na-rih-KOT-oh-mee): A site located in the Lake Turkana region of Kenya, where Turkana Boy was found.

neolithic: Belonging to the last phase of the Stone Age when agriculture was practiced.

nuclear DNA: Genetic material found in the cell's nucleus.

occupation site: A place where hominins gathered to dwell in or to perform an activity such as make tools or butcher an animal.

ocher (OH-kur): Yellow, brown, or red mineral-rich earth that is often used as pigment.

Olduvai (awl-doo-VYE) Gorge: Nicknamed the Cradle of Mankind, this fossil-rich site is in the Great Rift Valley of Tanzania, eastern Africa.

Olduvai (awl-doo-VYE) pick: A tool with a nail protruding from a wooden handle, which fits in the palm of the excavator's hand, that is used to break up packed surface dirt.

organism: Any form of life made up of individual parts that work together to carry out life processes.

out-of-Africa theory: A theory of human origins that proposes that modern humans evolved in Africa and then spread throughout the world.

Pacific Rim theory: A theory that the first immigrants into the Americas came by boat from Alaska, hugging the Pacific coastline.

paleoanthropology: The study of the ancient origins and behavior, as well as the ancient cultural, physical, and social development of humans.

paleobotanist: A person who studies ancient plant life.

paleogenetics: The study of ancient heredity.

Paleo-Indian: Meaning "ancient Indian," Paleo-Indians were the hunter-gatherers who first discovered the Americas.

Paleolithic: The cultural period of the Stone Age beginning with the development of the earliest stone tools. Sometimes called the Old Stone Age.

paleopathologist: A person who studies ancient disease.

pelvic bone: Hipbone.

periwinkle shells: The shells of sea snails.

photosynthesis: The process in green plants where carbohydrates are synthesized from carbon dioxide and water using light as an energy source.

physical anthropology: The branch of anthropology that deals with human evolutionary biology, physical variation, and classification.

physiology: The branch of biology that is concerned with the processes or functions in a living form.

pollen: The fine powdery fertilizing material of plants.

potassium: A metal component of bone.

prehistorian: A person who studies human and pre-human societies of the period before recorded history.

prehistoric: Before recorded history.

radioactive isotope: An atom with an unstable nucleus.

radiocarbon dating: A method of determining the age of an organic object by measuring the radioactivity present in the carbon of the object.

rickets: A bone disease caused by the lack of vitamin D.

robust: Powerfully built.

sacrum: A triangular bone of the pelvis.

***Salvadora* tree:** A small tree or shrub with a crooked trunk. Also called a toothbrush tree.

sediment: Material that settles at the bottom of liquid.

Shanidar Cave: A cave in Iraq that is famous for being the site where nine Neandertal skeletons were recovered.

sieving: The process of sifting dirt to find bones, teeth, artifacts, and anything else of interest to archaeologists.

silica: Material (sand or quartz) used in the manufacture of glass.

skull: The cranium, which protects the brain and the bones of the face.

sphincter (SFINGK-tur) muscles: O-shaped muscles that contract or close a bodily opening.

stromatolite: Dome-shaped structure composed of sediment and fossilized algae.

sub-adult: An individual who is no longer juvenile but not yet fully adult.

thoracic vertebra: The twelve vertebrae that make up the middle of the backbone.

tibia: The larger of the two bones from the knee to the ankle.

vervet monkey: An African guenon monkey. Scientists studied vervets to learn more about their vocalizations.

Wernicke's area: An area of the brain associated with language development.

Hominins and friends

(chapter references in parentheses)

Sir Walter Bodmer: German-born British geneticist. (Iceman)

David Brill: National Geographic photographer whose lens captured much of the dig at the Turkana Boy site.

Paul Broca: Nineteenth-century French surgeon and anthropologist who made many contributions toward the understanding of the anatomy of the brain. (Turkana Boy)

Luigi Luca Cavalli-Sforza: Italian-born American population geneticist. (Iceman)

James Chatters: American anthropologist who first excavated and examined Kennewick Man.

Noam Chomsky: American linguist. (Turkana Boy)

Clovis People: A Paleo-Indian culture of North America associated with distinctive stone tools that were first discovered in Clovis, New Mexico. (Iceman)

Confederated Tribes of the Colville Reservation: American Indian tribe living in eastern Washington State that tried to reclaim Kennewick Man's remains for their tribe.

Charles Darwin: English naturalist who was one of the first to publish evidence that all species have evolved over time from common ancestors through the process of natural selection. (Kennewick Man)

Cidália Duarte: Portuguese archaeologist who excavated the skeleton of Lapedo Child.

Markus Egg: German archaeologist overseeing the restoration of Iceman's belongings.

Pedro Ferreira: Portuguese student who found rock art in the Lapedo Valley that led to the discovery of Lapedo Child.

Rainer Henn: Head of the forensic team that examined Iceman's body.

Jane Hurst: British professor of animal science specializing in mammal communication. (Turkana Boy)

Iceman: Also known as Ötzi, Iceman is the well-preserved 5,300-year-old, modern human corpse that was found in the Alps in 1991.

Kamoya Kimeu: A Kenyan fossil hunter and leader of the Hominid Gang, who discovered many of the world's most important archaeological finds, including Turkana Boy.

Kanzi: Meaning "treasure" in Swahili, Kanzi is a male bonobo and the first ape to demonstrate true comprehension of language. (Turkana Boy)

Kennewick Man: The name given to the skeleton of a 9,000-year-old modern human that was found in 1996 on the bank of the Columbia River in the state of Washington.

Anton Koler: Austrian policeman and member of the mountain rescue team that recovered Iceman's remains.

Lapedo Child: Name given to the skeleton of a four-year-old child who was buried 25,000 years ago in the Lapedo Valley in Portugal.

Mary Leakey: British archaeologist and anthropologist and mother to Richard Leakey. (Turkana Boy)

Meave Leakey: British paleontologist whose field of study is human origins in Africa. She is also Richard Leakey's wife and accompanied him on the Turkana Boy dig.

Louise Leakey: Kenyan palenotologist. She is the daughter of Meave and Richard Leakey, and accompanied them on the Turkana Boy dig when she was twelve.

Richard Leakey: Kenyan paleontologist whose field of study is human origins in Africa. He is the son of Louis and Mary Leakey, husband of Meave Leakey, and father of Louise and Samira Leakey. Richard was the leader of the Turkana Boy dig team.

Samira Leakey: Child of Meave and Richard Leakey, she accompanied them on the Turkana Boy dig when she was ten.

Craig Littrell: The police sergeant in charge of Kennewick Man's "murder" investigation.

Catherine MacMillan: A physical anthropologist and owner of the consulting business The Bone-Apart Agency, MacMillan was a consultant on the Kennewick Man case.

Matata: Meaning "worries" in Swahili, Matata was a bonobo ape and mother to Kanzi. (Turkana Boy)

Reinhold Messner: An Italian mountaineer and explorer. He started a media buzz of theories about the Iceman find.

Klaus Oeggl: Austrian archaeobotonist who ran tests on a piece of Iceman's colon, hoping to be able to reconstruct the environment in which Iceman lived.

Ötzi: Also known as Iceman, Ötzi is the well-preserved 5,300-year-old, modern human corpse that was found in the Alps in 1991.

Doug Owsley: Forensic anthropologist for the Smithsonian Institution. (Kennewick Man)

Svante Pääbo: Swedish biologist specializing in evolutionary genetics. (Turkana Boy, Lapedo Child)

Steven Pinker: Canadian-American scientist specializing in language development. (Turkana Boy)

Sue Savage-Rumbaugh: American primatologist famous for her work with Great Ape language. (Turkana Boy)

Erika and Helmut Simon: German hikers who discovered Iceman in the Austrian-Italian Alps.

Bryan Sykes: British geneticist who specializes in human populations and their origins. He was able to recover DNA from Iceman's bones.

Will Thomas and Dave Deacy: The students who discovered Kennewick Man in the Columbia River in Washington state.

Erik Trinkaus: American paleoanthropologist who specializes in Neandertal biology and human origins. He joined João Zilhão and Cidália Duarte in the Lapedo Child research.

Turkana Boy: The name given to the almost complete 1.6-million-year-old skeleton of a *Homo erectus* boy found in Kenya in 1984.

Eduard Egarter Vigl: Italian pathologist in charge of the preservation of Iceman.

Alan Walker: British-born American paleoanthropologist who specializes in primate and human evolution. He joined Richard Leakey's team on the Turkana Boy dig and lead the laboratory team.

João Zilhão: Portuguese archaeologist and director of the Portuguese Institute of Archaeology. He was the leader of the team on the Lapedo Child dig.

Bibliography

Turkana Boy

Arsuaga, Juan Luis, and Ignacio Martínez. *The Chosen Species: The Long March of Human Evolution*. Malden, MA: Blackwell Publishing, 1998.

Darwin, Charles. *The Origin of Species by Means of Natural Selection*. London: J. Murray, 1859.

Diamond, Jared. *The Third Chimpanzee: The Evolution and Future of the Human Animal*. New York: HarperCollins, 1992.

Leakey, Richard, and Roger Lewin. *Origins Reconsidered: In Search of What Makes Us Human*. New York: Doubleday, 1992.

Lynch, John, and Louise Barrett. *Walking with Cavemen: Eye-to-Eye with Your Ancestors*. New York: DK Publishing, 2003.

Mithen, Steven. *The Singing Neanderthals*. Cambridge, MA: Harvard University Press, 2006.

Morell, Virginia. *Ancestral Passion: The Leakey Family and the Quest for Humankind's Beginning*. New York: Simon & Schuster, 1995.

Savage-Rumbaugh, Sue and Roger Lewin. *Kanzi: The Ape at the Brink of the Human Mind*. New York: Wiley, 1994.

Savage-Rumbaugh, Sue and Stuart G. Shanker and Talbot J. Taylor. *Apes, Language, and the Human Mind*. New York: Oxford University Press, 1998.

Schick, Kathy D., and Nicholas Toth. *Making Silent Stones Speak: Human Evolution and the Dawn of Technology*. New York: Simon & Schuster, 1993.

Tattersall, Ian. *Becoming Human: Evolution and Human Uniqueness*. New York: Harcourt Brace, 1998.

Tattersall, Ian. *The Fossil Trail: How We Know What We Think We Know About Human Evolution*. New York: Oxford University Press, 1995.

Wade, Nicholas. *Before the Dawn: Recovering the Lost History of Our Ancestors*. New York: Penguin, 2006.

Walker, Alan, and Pat Shipman. *The Wisdom of the Bones: In Search of Human Origins*. London: Weidenfeld and Nicolson, 1996.

Willis, Delta. *The Hominid Gang: Behind the Scenes in the Search of Human Origins*. New York: Viking, 1989.

From the World Wide Web

ACP-Monkeys>Vervets
http://www.acp.eugraph.com/monkey/index.html

"Animal Language Article"
http://www.santafe.edu/~johnson/articles.chimp.html

"Bridges to human language"
    http://www.drmillslmu.com/EVOLPSYC/fall99/panel5.htm
Human Origins/Evolution/DISCOVER Magazine
    http://www.discovermagazine.com/2003/jan/origins
Neanderthal Man/Science & Nature/Smithsonian Magazine
    http://www.smithsonianmag.com/science-nature/neanderthal.html
Origins of Language
    http://www.ship.edu/~cgboeree/langorigins.html
A Voluble Visit with Two Talking Apes—NPR
    http://www.npr.org/templates/story/story.php?storyID=5503685

Lapedo Child

Dumiak, Michael. "The Neanderthal Code." *Archaeology,*
    November/December 2006, pp. 22–25.
Johanson, Donald, and Lenora Johanson. *Ancestors: In Search of Human
    Origins.* New York: Villard Books, 1994.
Klein, Richard G., and Blake Edgar. *The Dawn of Culture.* New York:
    Wiley, 2002.
Kunzig, Robert. "Learning to Love Neanderthals." *Discover* 20 (8), August
    1999.
Shreeve, James. *The Neandertal Enigma: Solving the Mystery of Human
    Origins.* New York: William Morrow and Company, 1995.
Trinkaus, Erik, and Pat Shipman. *The Neandertals: Changing the Image of
    Mankind.* New York: Knopf, 1993.
Zilhão, João, and Erik Trinkaus. *Portrait of the Artist as a Child: The
    Gravettian Human Skeleton from the Abrigo do Lagar Velho and its
    Archeological Context.* Lisboa, Portugal: Instituto Português de
    Arqueologia, 2002.

From the World Wide Web

BBC NEWS/Science/Nature/Cave fossils are early Europeans
    http://news.bbc.co.uk/go/pr/fr/-/2/hi/science/nature/6099422.stm
Discovery Channel: Archaeology: Skull Shows Human-Neanderthal Link
    http://dsc.discovery.com/news/2007/01/16/neanderthal_arc.html?
    category=archaeology&guid=20070116104530
Neanderthal Man/Science & Nature/Smithsonian Magazine
    http://www.smithsonianmag.com/science-nature/neanderthal.htm

Kennewick Man

Chatters, James C. *Ancient Encounters: Kennewick Man and the First
    Americans.* New York: Simon & Schuster, 2001.
Downey, Roger. *Riddle of the Bones: Politics, Science, Race, and the Story of
    Kennewick Man.* New York: Copernicus, 2000.

Fagan, Brian. *People of the Earth: An Introduction to World Prehistory.* New York: HarperCollins, 1992.

Oakes, Ted. *Land of Lost Monsters: Man against Beast: The Prehistoric Battle for the Planet.* New York. Hydra, 2003.

Olson, Steve. *Mapping Human History: Discovering the Past Through our Genes.* New York: Houghton Mifflin, 2002.

Tankersley, Kenneth. *In Search of Ice Age Americans.* Salt Lake City: Gibbs Smith, 2002.

Thomas, David Hurt. *Skull Wars: Kennewick Man, Archaeology, and the Battle for Native American Identity.* New York: Basic Books, 2000.

Ward, Peter D. *The Call of Distant Mammoths: Why the Ice Age Mammals Disappeared.* New York: Copernicus, 1997.

Wells, Spencer. *The Journey of Man: A Genetic Odyssey.* New York: Random House, 2004.

Ziff, Bruce H. and Pratima V. Rao. *Borrowed Power: Essays on Cultural Appropriation.* New Brunswick, NJ: Rutgers University Press, 1997.

From the World Wide Web

Battle over Kennewick Man appears over—Science-msnbc.com
http://www.msnbc.msn.com/id/5456191/

BBC News/Americas/Science wins ancient bones battle
http://news.bbc.co.uk/2/hi/americas/3460773.stm

Bones tell ancient tale of Kennewick Man—Science-msnbc.com
http://www.msnbc.msn.com/id/11532671/

Friends of America's Past: Forum: A Conversation with James Chatters
http://www.friendsofpast.org/forum/chatters-conversation.html

JS Online: Teeth could tell fossil's tale
http://www3.jsonline.com/story/index.aspx?id=389315

Kenan Malik's essay
http://www.kenanmalik.com/essays/index_knowledge.html

Kennewick Man—Burke Museum
http://www.washington.edu/burkemuseum/kman/native_american_views.php

Kennewick Man/Tri-City Herald: Mid-Columbia news
http://www.tri-cityherald.com/kman/

The last days of Kennewick Man [Archive]—Vanguard News Network
http://www.vnnforum.com/archive/index.php/t-30127.html

Local News/Kennewick Man yields ancient secrets/Seattle Times
http://community.seattletimes.nwsource.com/archive/date=20050711&slug=kennewick11m

Scientists win Kennewick Man ruling
http://www.seattlepi.com/local/159408_kennewickman05.html

Who Were the First Americans?—TIME
http://www.time.com/time/magazine/article/0,9171,1169905-1,00.html

Iceman

Diamond, Jared. *Guns, Germs, and Steel: The Fates of Human Societies.* New York: Norton, 1999.

Feder, Kenneth L. *The Past In Perspective: An Introduction to Human Prehistory.* Mountain View, CA: Mayfield, 2000.

Fowler, Brenda. *Iceman: Uncovering the Life and Times of a Prehistoric Man Found in an Alpine Glacier.* Chicago: University of Chicago Press, 2000.

Olson, Steve. *Mapping Human History.*

Spindler, Konrad. *The Man in the Ice: The Discovery of a 5,000-Year-Old Body Reveals the Secrets of the Stone Age.* New York: Harmony Books, 1994.

Sykes, Bryan. *The Seven Daughters of Eve: The Science That Reveals Our Genetic Ancestry.* New York: Norton, 2001.

Thorpe, I. J. *The Origins of Agriculture in Europe.* New York: Routledge, 1999.

From the World Wide Web

BBC—Science & Nature—Horizon—Death of the Iceman—Transcript
http://www.bbc.co.uk/science/horizon/2001/icemantrans.shtml

Iceman
http://www.american.edu/TED/iceman.htm

New Research on Ötzi, the Iceman, Cometh < Anthropology.net
http://anthropology.net/2007/03/20/new-research-on-otzi-the-iceman-cometh/

News in Science—Arrow wound killed Ötzi the iceman
http://www.abc.net.au/science/news/stories/2007/1944943.htm

A Unique Find/Ötzi—South Tyrol Museum of Archaeology
http://www.archaeologiemuseum.it/en/oetzi-the-iceman

Archaeology

Bahn, Paul. *Written in the Bones: How Human Remains Unlock the Secrets of the Dead.* Toronto: Firefly Books, 2003.

Dillehay, Thomas. *The Settlement of the Americas: A New Prehistory.* New York: Basic, 2000.

Renfrew, Colin, and Paul Bahn. *Archaeology Essentials: Theories, Methods, and Practice.* London: Thames and Hudson, 2007.

Tracing human ancestry

Klein, Richard G. *The Human Career.* Chicago: University of Chicago Press, 1999.

Robertshaw, Peter and Jill Rubalcaba. *The Early Human World.* New York: Oxford University Press, 2004.

Index

Acknowledgments

We'd like to express our gratitude to the following people who contributed generously to this project: Wes Niewoehner for expert advice and encouragement. Alan Walker and Jim Chatters for their generous assistance in providing photographs of their work. Erik Trinkaus for advice on the Lapedo Child. Tonia Boughamer for her hard work in helping us find photos. Matt Wuerker for permitting us to reproduce his "Skull Wars" cartoon. The South Tyrol Museum of Archaeology for their contribution of Iceman images. Editor extraordinaire, Randi Rivers, who shaped this book from the very beginning and who patiently and cheerfully kept us on track throughout. Copyeditor, Josette Haddad, for skillfully ferreting out our flaws. Susan Sherman for art direction and design. Ginger Knowlton for handling the business end with aplomb. And a special thanks to our families who encourage and support us in all our endeavors.

Photo credits

Jacket

Photograph by James Chatters, front; Photograph courtesy of Alan Walker, back

Photograph courtesy of Instituto de Gestao do Património Arquitectónico e Arqueológico, IP (IGESPAR), p. i; Photograph courtesy of Instituto de Gestao do Património Arquitectónico e Arqueológico, IP (IGESPAR), p. ii (top); Photograph courtesy of Alan Walker, p. ii (middle); Photograph © by South Tyrol Museum of Archaeology. www.iceman.it, p. ii (bottom); Photograph by James Chatters, p. iii

Turkana Boy

Illustration from NIH pub. no. 97-4257, October 2008, http://www.nidcd.nih.gov/health/voice/aphasia.asp, p. 33; all other photographs in this section are courtesy of Alan Walker

Lapedo Child

All photographs in this section are courtesy of Instituto de Gestao do Património Arquitectónico e Arqueológico, IP (IGESPAR)

Kennewick Man

Photograph by Jennifer Elf, p. 107; Illustration © Matt Wuerker, p. 113; Photograph by Jennifer Elf, p. 119; all other photographs in this section are by James Chatters

Iceman

Photograph courtesy of Roger Teissl, p. 129; Photograph © by S.N.S./Sipa Press, p. 136; Photograph courtesy of Klaus Oeggl, Botanical Institute, University of Innsbruck, p. 150; "The spread of agriculture in Europe and west Asia" illustration courtesy of Dr. Dorian Fuller (UCL Institute of Archaeology), p. 161; all other photographs in this section are © by South Tyrol Museum of Archaeology. www.iceman.it

Photograph courtesy of Alan Walker, p. 176 (bottom); Photograph courtesy of Instituto de Gestao do Património Arquitectónico e Arqueológico, IP (IGESPAR), 176 (top); Photograph by James Chatters, p. 177 (top left); Photograph © by South Tyrol Museum of Archaeology. www.iceman.it, p. 177 (top right)